Thomas Bray's
Grand Design

ACRL Publications in Librarianship no. 35

Thomas Bray's Grand Design

Libraries of the Church of England in America, 1695-1785

by
Charles T. Laugher

AMERICAN LIBRARY ASSOCIATION
Chicago 1973

Association of College and
Research Libraries

Publications in Librarianship

Editor Edward G. Holley

Library of Congress Cataloging in Publication Data

Laugher, Charles T
Thomas Bray's grand design.

(ACRL publications in librarianship, no. 35)
Includes bibliographical references.
1. Libraries—United States—History,
2. Bray, Thomas, 1658-1730. 3. Church of
England in America. I. Title. II. Series:
Association of College and Research Libraries.
ACRL publications in librarianship, no. 35.
Z674.A75 no. 35 [Z731] 021′.00973 73-16332
ISBN 0-8389-0151-4

For my children

Contents

Preface

My interest in Thomas Bray and his plans for American libraries began several years ago, in North Carolina, when I first learned of the "Public Library of the Province" established by law in 1705 at Bath. As my interest in the man and his work grew, I quickly discovered how little information was readily available concerning him in print, except for the excellent article by Bernard C. Steiner on Maryland libraries which appeared in *The American Historical Review* in 1896–97.

The lack of attention paid to Bray is amazing, considering that he, together with the societies he established to carry on his work, laid the foundation for nearly one hundred libraries in America between 1695 and 1785, and continued to supply ministers, teachers, and books to the colonies until the Revolution.

Later, while doing research for a dissertation on Bray at Case Western Reserve University, I was able to obtain a copy of his account books covering the years 1695–1704 from C. Hoare and Company, a London bank founded by one of the original members of the Society for the Promotion of Christian Knowledge. These records were more complete than the other two known copies and provided a great deal of information about the cost of the libraries, catalogs of their contents, and the names of the cities and towns to which they were sent.

It is hoped that this description of Bray's libraries will encourage further research to increase our understanding of this selfless and dedicated man, who did so much to alleviate the intellectual poverty of colonial America.

I would like to thank the Trustees of Amherst College, who gave me a sabbatical leave to complete revision; Dr. Edward G. Holley, Chairman of the ACRL Publications board when this manuscript was accepted; and the members of the Editorial staff of the American Library Association, who did what they could to help me improve the work. Despite this assistance, the writer alone is responsible for any errors remaining in the finished product.

Chapter 1
Introduction: The Colonial Scene

Colonial settlers in seventeenth-century America lived at a time when denominational religion was still of vital importance in men's lives. The church was a town's leading institution, the focal point of all intellectual and social life. The clergy often shared political control with the magistrates, since they were entrusted by the Bible with the exercise of moral discipline; they were highly respected by those who directed trade and commerce, and exerted an influence almost incomprehensible today. As the representatives of a vested interest that, in theory at least, admitted to no separation between church and state, the clergy acted as a force for social discipline, promoting conservatism and stability.

The Protestant denominations, often with only minor differences in doctrine or discipline, predominated in all of the colonies. In fact until the beginning of the eighteenth century, when the emergence of numerous rival sects caused a weakening in the power of the established churches (such as the Congregational churches of New England and the Church of England in some of the Middle and Southern colonies), these churches exerted considerable influence in all phases of colonial life. The rapid spread of the Church of England in the eighteenth century in the colonies, for example, greatly altered the religious complexion of New England. Under royal and official patronage, Anglicanism offered a religious atmosphere warmer and more colorful than the narrow severity of early Congregationalism or the austerity of the Friends.

The physical growth of cities and the burst of commercial expansion in the colonies led to an increase in wealth and leisure, and religion was forced to broaden its outlook to encompass the new complexities of the social order. With the growth of materialism, in fact, the churches often had to share the leisure time of the colonists with taverns and coffeehouses. The Church of England, serving the leaders of society and the newly

1

wealthy members of the middle class, did increase in popularity, but as commercial success altered the singleness of purpose and outlook of the colonists by acquainting them with secular pleasures and offering the leisure and wealth to enjoy them, all churches found their powers ebbing away.

From the beginning, books filled an important need in the lives of the American colonists. Few public libraries—libraries owned by a public body such as a church, town, or college—existed in seventeenth-century America. A town library was started in Boston by Robert Keayne, who at his death in 1656 bequeathed to the town his "three great writing books," along with such of his "Divinitie bookes and commentaries" as the ministers should think suitable for a public library. Another addition came in 1674, when the Reverend John Wilson bequeathed ten volumes. In 1702 John Barnard was directed to make a catalog of the collection and take two duplicate books as a reward. The Town House and its library were destroyed by fire in 1711, but despite some losses, most of the books were saved and carefully reassembled by the selectmen. In 1734 a group of subscribers, headed by Colonel Thomas Finch, made a considerable donation for the acquisition of new volumes for the collection. It is doubtful, however, that the library ever amounted to much more than a small collection of theology.[1]

New Haven began a town library with a gift of books from Governor Eaton and his brother. This collection was sold to James Pierpont in 1689, and the majority of the books eventually found their way to the Yale collection.[2]

Harvard College had the largest collection of books in North America at the end of the seventeenth century. By 1723, when the first catalog was printed, the library contained some 3,500 volumes, 2,183 of which were related to theology.[3]

When the Massachusetts Bay colonists, dissatisfied with the living conditions at Cambridge, decided to move across the river to the present site of Boston, they found an eccentric Anglican clergyman named William Blackstone in residence on the peninsula of Shawmut. In his *Magnalia*, Cotton Mather spoke of "Blaxton" as one reckoned among the "godly Epescopalians," and referred to him as one who "happened to sleep in a hovel upon a patch of land there," and laid claim to "all the ground whereupon there now stands the metropolis of the whole English America, until the inhabitants gave him satisfaction."[4]

Blackstone sold his land to the Puritans and moved to Rhode Island, settling on the Blackstone River some six miles north of Providence. The inventory of his "Lands, Goods and Chattels," dated May 28, 1675, shows that his library consisted of "three Bibles, three Latin Books in Folio, eight ditto in large quarto, twenty-nine small quarto, thirty large octavo, twenty-five small ditto, ten paper books." A note in the margin relates that "this estate was destroyed or carried away by the Natives."[5]

2

Many of the early settlers of New England, notably John Winthrop and Edward Tyng, brought libraries with them to America. As early as 1637 one "Saunders" opened a "Bookbynder" shop in Boston, and in 1647 Hezekiah Usher began importing books for sale. The presence of an excellent book market in New England is evident; between 1669 and 1690, for instance, twenty booksellers had shops in Boston, most of them clustered around the Town House. One of John Usher's invoices for 1685 gives an idea of the literary diet of the Bostonians: of 874 titles, 391 were school texts, 311 were religious works, 55 were Bibles, 50 were books on navigation, 36 were law books, and the remaining 21 were concerned with medicine, history, military science, and romance.[6]

In the Middle and Southern colonies, records indicate that books were equally important in the lives of the colonists there. In the New Netherlands the Dutch, although long thought to be a purely commercial group, developed literary tendencies early, strengthened by close ties with the mother country. Dutch colonists placed a strong emphasis on the importance of a learned clergy, and as a consequence, many colonists owned libraries, notably the Rensselaers and Jonas Bronck, a wealthy merchant.

The Swedes, for the short time they held a foothold along the Delaware, produced several literary works dealing with the New World. Jesper Svedberg, the father of the great Emanuel, wrote *America Illuminata* to acquaint his countrymen with America.[7] John Campanius Holm and Israel Acrelius wrote large and fully descriptive works, which for minuteness of treatment were not surpassed by any other writers in the entire period.[8] Of the three, Acrelius alone actually lived in America and wrote from firsthand experience. In his fresh and interesting treatment, Acrelius relates perhaps the first account of an attempt to found parochial libraries in America: In 1693 Charles Springer wrote from the Delaware asking Postmaster Thalin of Göteborg for 12 Bibles, 3 collections of sermons, 42 manuals, 100 handbooks and spiritual meditations, 200 catechisms, and 200 "ABC books." In the following year he wrote for 3 postils, 13 Bibles, and 21 manuals, and appended a list of the names of the men who had agreed to pay for the books in case of loss or accident.[9]

King Carl XI sent a selection of books to three clergymen who were setting out for America in 1694 as a donation to their congregations. These books included 500 copies of Luther, Bibles, postils, and other church books, all with the king's initials stamped on the covers in gold. The king continued to send books to the Swedish settlements along the Delaware from 1694 to 1748; in all he sent over 1,000 volumes.[10]

Any discussion of the development of American intellectual life inevitably centers on the English-speaking colonies, especially Virginia and Massachusetts, as they gave form to the culture and society which eventually developed along the entire seaboard, from Maine to the Carolinas.

That the so-called Virginia Cavaliers were vitally interested in religion and theology is a point not generally stressed by historians. Stereotypes usually contrast the materialistic, pleasure-loving Southerner with New England's narrow, ascetic Puritan, preoccupied with involved theological points. Recent studies of seventeenth- and eighteenth-century libraries in the South, however, indicate that Southerners, too, owned a large proportion of theological works. Apparently the reading habits of colonial Americans were quite similar throughout the British colonies at the end of the seventeenth and beginning of the eighteenth centuries. As James Truslow Adams said, "There was no noticable difference in the number of households in the North and South who had libraries," with the contents of the libraries "more nearly equal in 1700 than later."[11] Louis Wright also maintained that religious works continued to occupy a large place in Southern libraries during those two centuries, with an increase in general philosophical works and a decrease in works of simple piety as the eighteenth century advanced, although religion continued to maintain a place in these libraries throughout the entire period.[12]

It is certain that men in colonial times did not simply build expensive libraries for show. Books were dear then, especially when they had to be imported from England or the Continent. Books the colonists brought with them or purchased from abroad were thus carefully chosen to provide many kinds of guidance for the conditions found in the New World.

Contact between the mother country and the colonies was of vital importance at the end of the seventeenth century. The colonies were too new and small to stand alone. Land was abundant, labor scarce, and capital brought from home declined in value through depreciation of the colonial currencies. The immigrant was normally a poor man when he left home, whether evicted for political or religious reasons, or motivated by personal economic distress, and was on his own once he arrived. The enrichments of life at home, whether open to him or not, did not exist even for the wealthy in the New World.

The Anglican church stood in a special position among American denominations at that time because it was the established church not only of several of the colonies, but of the mother country as well. Throughout the colonies, the Anglican clergyman served as an important link between the religious and cultural life of England and that of the transatlantic settlements. The ministry and two great religious societies, the Society for the Promotion of Christian Knowledge and the Society for the Propagation of the Gospel in Foreign Parts, strived to fill the vacuum which the trader, military man, or royal governor could not hope to fill. Thus it was the clergy who represented education and learning in the eighteenth century when the man of culture and leisure no longer felt compelled to cross the seas.

The home government never saw fit to authorize a resident bishop for the New World. Instead, the churches and their clergy were under jurisdiction of the Bishop of London. The absence of a bishop in the colonies meant that no priest could be ordained in America; consequently, every minister serving in the colonies had to be either a native of the British Isles, ordained there before his departure for America, or a colonial who had made the expensive and hazardous voyage to England for his education and ordination.

Thomas Bray and the Society for the Propagation of the Gospel in Foreign Parts played a large part in fostering strong ties between the colonies and the mother country. By supplying missionaries, paying their salaries, and sending forth a steady stream of books for their libraries, the Society shared in the intellectual development of the colonies for over 100 years. The genius of Thomas Bray and his successors in the religious societies lay in their complete understanding of the frontier problem of intellectual poverty, and the steps they took to remedy this poverty of mind and soul. "No body of men has ever more thoroughly analyzed the spiritual or intellectual needs of a new society than did Thomas Bray and his associates."[13]

The main objective of these societies was the equalization of Christian culture on both sides of the Atlantic; to accomplish this feat, libraries were provided, schools established, and a steady stream of teachers, missionaries, and clergymen maintained for nearly a century. These men attempted to solidly establish local churches and schools so as to make them independent of any missionary support. The societies appealed for funds throughout England, arguing that it was only good business to raise the religious and cultural level of the colonies, which had reverted to primitivism in the opinion of many clergymen. Such a disaster, besides being an obvious spiritual loss, would also have brought about a deterioration of citizenship, making the business relationships between the colonies and England precarious.

When ministers were sent to America by the Society for the Propagation of the Gospel in Foreign Parts, they went not as missionaries in the strictest sense of the word, but instead as men invited by a congregation after it had become large enough to raise a church and was able to partially support a clergyman. The motto of the Society clearly expresses this: *Transiens adjuva nos*, "come over and help us."

At a time in which a book was a treasured heirloom, and a single shelf of the old secretary could hold the entire literary possessions of several generations, the establishment of libraries was vital for the foundation of any intellectual life. The requests for books which fill entire pages of the S.P.G. letter books vividly express the keen hunger of the colonists for literature from the mother country. The libraries sent by Bray and the Society were not regarded simply as gifts, in fact, but as an indispensable factor in inducing men of education to move to the colonies. In addition to the libraries, therefore, each minister was given chests of books for his use and that of his parishioners "unto all future generations." The careful instructions included with the libraries for cataloging the books to prevent loss and "embezlment" were not made to impede circulation, but to instill a feeling of respect and value in the user; Bray wrote that one of the advantages of a lending library was that "a Book which is lent is more speedily read over and better digested than books of their [the user's] own."[14]

A great number of the titles in these libraries were, of course, religious, concerned with theological points and doctrinal disputes. But Bray was also convinced that a thoroughly educated clergyman must be equally interested in works of natural religion and moral philosophy, as well as the "Various and different Oeconomics." Like Milton, he felt that education of the people would destroy atheism; like Defoe, that it would dispel idleness.

Of special necessity and value to the preparation of American missionaries were books of biography, voyages, and travels. Books of nature provided the churchman with a weapon against the Deists, since such knowledge could be used for good, as well as evil, purposes. Likewise, the virulent books written by enemies of the Established Church required careful reading, "For as the Excellent Plutarch shows, the best Rules and Measures for an exact and Prudent Conduct are to be taken from our enemies, who do so narrowly watch our Failings."[15]

The caliber of men sent to the colonies was generally excellent, as the completeness of their reports, preserved in the S.P.G. archives, amply testifies. In excess of 50,000 manuscript pages provides a mine of information on the American character, the processes of Americanization, and the broad development of American culture. Observations on plant and animal life, agriculture and business, prices and colonial currency, intercolonial communication, the transit of ideas, growth of population, racial relations with Negroes and Indians, and contacts with other, newly arrived national groups are included. These men obviously observed the people and the country carefully.

Stemming from the Church of England, indeed from all the colonial churches to some degree, were influences helping to build a practical democracy composed of humanitarianism, civil liberty, tolerance, and private benevolence which established hospitals, schools, colleges, missionary societies, and philanthropic enterprises. America, which derives so largely from seventeenth- and eighteenth-century England, owes a great debt of gratitude to Thomas Bray and the societies he founded.

Thus it was within this colonial framework, in which books were scarce and found mainly within the churches, that the first concerted effort to establish libraries on a large scale was instituted for the people of the New World, from Newfoundland to the West Indies. Probably few men have realized the power of the book, or the necessity of bringing that power to the people, more fully than Thomas Bray; the remains of his libraries still stand today, a lasting tribute to the noble and dedicated man who would have asked for nothing more.

Chapter 2
Thomas Bray

Thomas Bray was born in the hamlet of Marton, Shropshire, in 1658.[1] His family was poor but of good standing in the community. Thomas showed early promise of scholarly attainment, but probably would have been denied an education save that his interest and aptitude for learning brought him to the attention of Edward Lewis, the vicar of Chirbury, a town three miles from Marton. Lewis possessed a remarkable collection of chained books, and encouraged the young scholar to use them. (In the early days of printing when books were expensive and scarce, they were often chained to the shelf to prevent theft.) He bequeathed his collection to the Chirbury school in 1677; William Blades, in his 1892 survey, described the library as amounting to over 200 volumes.[2]

Bray's Education

It is probable that Lewis encouraged Bray's parents to send him to Oswestry Grammar School to prepare for a university education. From Oswestry he matriculated at All Souls College, Oxford, in March, 1674/75, as a *puer pauper*, supporting himself by menial service to the Fellows.[3] He was graduated with a Bachelor of Arts degree in 1678, but could not immediately afford to remain at the College as a Fellow, which was necessary if he wished to proceed to the Master of Arts degree. He finally took his Master of Arts degree in 1693 from Hart Hall, a change of schools necessitated because of his failure to secure a fellowship at All Souls. In 1696, largely because Governor Nicholson and the Council of Maryland thought it would improve his position with the colonial clergy, he advanced to the degree of Bachelor of Divinity and Doctor of Divinity from Magdalen College.

He was ordained a deacon in 1681 and appointed to a parish near Bridgnorth, in Warwickshire, where he came to the attention of Sir Thomas

Price of Park Hall. This gentleman made him his chaplain and secured for him the living of Lea Marsten, where he served until 1689. Living nearby was a staunch nonjuror, John Kettlewell, vicar of Coleshill, who had been presented that living by Simon, Lord Digby. (Unlike most of the clergymen who refused to swear allegiance to King William, Kettlewell was not deprived of his living.) Each year when the county court sessions, or assizes, were held, a local clergyman was chosen to give the opening sermon. Through his friendship with Kettlewell, Bray came to the attention of Lord Digby, and when he was chosen to preach the assize sermon at Warwich, Digby was in the audience. He was so impressed with the young priest's dedication that he recommended Bray to his brother William, who soon after offered him the living of Over Whitacre. While at Whitacre, Bray married, but nothing is known of his wife save her name, Elenor. She bore him two children, Goditha and William, and the vestry records show she died in 1689.[4] William became a publisher and bookseller in London, and Goditha married a rich upholsterer named Martin, supported many of her father's schemes, and was financially responsible for the publication of the earliest biography of her father, *Public Spirit*, said to have been written by Bray's friend and executor Samuel Smith.

In 1690, William Digby presented Bray with the rectory of Sheldon, made vacant when the Reverend Digby Bull refused to take the oath of allegiance to the king. Bray continued to hold that living until his death in 1730, though a curate served the parish for a number of years.

Missionary Work

One of Bray's earliest passions, which he continued throughout his life, was the encouragement of clerical studies aimed at teaching the clergy to catechize properly. In 1695, Archbishop Tenison, under Crown authority, had issued injunctions calling for the enforcement of the Fifty-ninth Canon on catechizing the young, which had been neglected since the Restoration. Early in 1696, Bray completed the first volume of his *Catechetical Lectures*. The lectures were dedicated to and published under the sponsorship of Dr. William Lloyd, Bishop of Coventry and Litchfield.[5] This first volume, containing over 300 pages, dealt solely with the first four questions and answers of the Common Prayer Book Catechism. He planned to continue the work in four volumes, but it was not until 1702 that the work was published in its complete form, in five parts.[6] The book could not have appeared at a more opportune time; because of the revived interest in catechizing, it was an instant success. The first edition of 3,000 copies was sold out and Bray realized a profit of £700.

Some writers believe that the publication of this work brought Bray to the attention of Bishop Compton of London, influencing the Bishop to appoint Bray as his commissary to the colony of Maryland, but a study of

Bray's own accounts shows that he was already engaged in work for Maryland in the fall of 1695, when he appointed a curate for Sheldon and moved to London. It is more probable that Bray came to the attention of Compton through his friendship with Bishop Lloyd and the Digbys. Further, the clergy in Maryland knew in May of 1696 that he had been appointed; in a letter to Bishop Compton, protesting their poverty, they spoke of looking forward to the coming of "the Reverend Dr. Bray, your Lordship's designed Commissary."[7]

Henry Compton, Bishop of London, had been concerned with the spiritual welfare of the colonies from the time he took office. In 1689 he had appointed James Blair as Commissary for Virginia. When he offered the Maryland appointment to Bray, the latter accepted on the condition that Compton and the other bishops support his plans to provide libraries for all the missionaries. The condition was accepted, and Bray went ahead with his plans, but circumstances did not permit the new commissary to begin his service until nearly four years later. In the interim Bray was far from idle: he began to select the missionaries and build up the libraries for the New World. His success seems to have impressed Colonel Nicholson, Governor of Maryland; in a letter written April 30, 1697, to the Bishop of London, he suggested that Bray be made commissary for New York, Pennsylvania, and New England as well as for Maryland.[8]

One of Bray's greatest problems was to obtain the funds necessary to support his schemes. Accompanied by Sir Thomas Lawrence, secretary of Maryland, Bray had an audience with Princess Anne and outlined a proposal that the capital of the new colony be named Annapolis in her honor. He also told her of his library plans, and she was so impressed that she made him a gift of forty guineas. As a result the first library was earmarked for Annapolis, and was nearly ready to send out by April of 1696.

As the missionary library plans went forward, Bray found that the clergy in England were also in need of books, and so began his work for the erection of parochial libraries in England and Wales, as outlined in his *Essay towards Promoting All Necessary and Useful Knowledge.* His work in finding acceptable ministers for America also continued, and in December, 1697, Bishop Compton held an ordination of missionaries in St. Paul's Cathedral, at which Bray preached the sermon published as *Apostolick Charity.*[9] Attached to the volume was a survey that Bray had made of conditions in the plantations, showing the number of churches, parishes, ministers, schools, and libraries. By this date sixteen libraries had been sent to Maryland, seven had been set up in the other colonies, and the foundations for six others had been laid. The completeness of this survey, published two years after his appointment, is an example of the thoroughness with which Bray pursued the designs important to him.

Through his interviews with candidates for appointment as missionaries he came to realize the difficulty in finding worthy men. Since clerical livings were relatively few in England due to the large number of candidates, only the poorer or less influential men applied for the hazardous voyage to the colonies. Such men could scarcely afford to support themselves, much less purchase a library. Bray intensified his efforts towards securing financial support for the missionaries through solicitation of funds and from support of wealthy or powerful friends. But dependence on friendship and donations was not enough, and he conceived a design for a chartered society. Because of the press of other duties, however, he could not immediately proceed with his plans, and settled finally for a voluntary society under the supervision of the bishops. This voluntary society came into existence in March of 1699 as the Society for the Promotion of Christian Knowledge.

Two preferments were offered to him in 1699: the office of Sub-Almoner, and the living of St. Botolph Aldgate, but he refused to consider them, feeling they would be incompatible with his position as commissary.

Commissary to Maryland

In 1699, Bray felt he could delay the voyage to Maryland no longer. To raise the passage money, he sold his furniture and some of his shares in the mining adventure of his friend, Humphrey Mackworth.[10] He set out from London on December 15, and arrived at Gravesend the next day. With his usual concern for the welfare of his fellowman, Bray presented that city with a library to be used by naval chaplains and other seagoing clergy to enrich the idle moments they were compelled to spend in that port. During the same week, he established libraries in the seaport towns of Plymouth and Deal.[11]

Bray's account of his voyage, recorded in his own hand in the manuscripts he eventually bequeathed to Sion College, contains interesting observations on the voyage, the conditions of travel, and his fellow passengers, most of whom did not meet with his approval. He set sail on the *Adventure* on January 4, 1700, and experienced an exceedingly stormy crossing. The ship was driven north to Newfoundland, where a short survey of the countryside left Bray wondering bitterly how a nation "professing Christianity in its purity" could fail to care for the religious needs of a colony of "so many 1000 Soules, who are all of them Natives of England," especially as their fishing trade, second in importance only to woolen manufacture, was great enough to turn the balance of European commerce in England's favor.

Without the knowledge of either Bray or Compton, the Act of Establishment had been defeated by the Quakers, who were opposed to paying a poll tax for the support of Anglican ministers, and ironically this news

11

was being secretly carried back to the Maryland Assembly by one of Bray's fellow passengers, a Quaker named Edward Singleton.[12] On his arrival at Annapolis, Bray found that Governor Nicholson had been transferred to Virginia, and Nathaniel Blakiston had replaced him in Maryland. When Bray presented himself to the new governor, he found that Singleton had already reported the defeat of the Act of Establishment. Blakiston promised to call the Assembly at once and draw up a new bill, before the Quakers could muster opposition. Nicholson came over from Virginia to offer his support, and he, along with Bray, Attorney-General Dent, and Speaker Smithson redrafted the act for establishing the Church. While waiting for the assembly to convene, Bray conducted a survey of church affairs in the colony. The results showed that a large proportion of the people were Anglicans. The Quakers, instead of constituting the majority they claimed before the Board of Trade, actually made up only about one-tenth of the population, with an estimated one-twelfth of the remainder Roman Catholic.[13]

On May 5, 1700, Bray preached a sermon before the Assembly on "The Necessity of an Early Religion," and the members passed a resolution of thanks for the "Excellent Sermon" with orders that it be printed.[14] Two days later, the Assembly passed the Act of Establishment, and the Assembly members recommended that Bray return to England with the bill to personally urge the king's approval. Before his departure, Bray called a general visitation of all the clergy of Maryland, and eighteen assembled in Annapolis on May 23. After he had given them his visitation charge, the clergy adopted resolutions thanking the Assembly and the governor for passing the bill. They joined with the Assembly in urging that Bray return immediately to England, where he could do more good for the Church. They also planned a visitation for the following year, which they "earnestly requested he would make among them personally."[15]

Bray thus set sail soon after the visitation and arrived in London on July 25, where he presented a memorial to the Society for the Promotion of Christian Knowledge, explaining his speedy return. He discovered that the Quakers had already organized strong opposition to the bill, and despite his active support it failed for the third time to gain the king's favor. Bray drafted a new bill himself, and, after three amendments, it was passed by the Board of Trade with the understanding that it must be sent to Maryland and passed by the Assembly without alteration. The king would then give it his approval.

Despite the continued opposition of the Quakers, who spent over £20,000 in their attempts to defeat the bill, it was finally passed by Parliament in 1701.[16] King William III signed the bill with the following comment: "Have the Quakers the benefit of Toleration? Let the Established Church have an Established Maintenance."[17] The new act gave toleration to the Quakers and Dissenters and provided a maintenance for every minister of a Church of England congregation in Maryland. That the law remained in force throughout Maryland's entire colonial period is a testimony to the stubbornness and zeal of the commissary.

Bray wrote several circular letters from England to the clergy of Maryland after the passage of the act, and from the second letter it is clear that he always intended to return to America. Finding that his affairs were likely to keep him in England for some time, however, he deputized several members of the Maryland clergy to hold visitations, visit the parishes, and oversee the libraries and churches until he could return. This same letter included as an appendix his plans for a layman's library, being "a lending Library for the use of the Laity."[18]

Among the affairs which acted to keep him in England were his plans for the chartered Society, which he had been forced to lay aside temporarily, and the simple necessity of making a living and supporting his family. On June 23, 1701, at a meeting of the Society for the Promotion of Christian Knowledge, he was able to present a charter for the new Society, signed by the king, before the members.[19]

Bray did not receive the money promised by the Maryland Assembly as his commissary salary since he had not remained in the colony long enough, but the Assembly did vote him £100 in appreciation for his services to them, and he duly entered the amount in his accounts under "Emoluments," stating that the money was "Presented me by the Assembly in the year 1699 and paid to Govr. Nicholson for me £100 their money which was reduced to ours an amount of £86." In addition, there were gifts from several of his friends which amounted to £80.7.6, also duly recorded.[20] Most of the money he received from Sheldon went to pay his curate, and his accounts show that during the years 1695 to 1702, he paid out a total of £79.12.6 more in renting a house for his family than he received in salary and gifts.

Because of his increased labors at home, Bray found that a return visit to Maryland was impossible, and so he persuaded Bishop Compton to appoint another commissary in his place. His chosen successor was the Reverend Michael Huitson, Archdeacon of Armagh, and as John Seymour, the governor of Maryland, happened to be in London at that time, Compton arranged a dinner at Fulham Palace so that Bray and Huitson could meet the new governor. During the course of the meal, Seymour became furious when Compton proposed that the right of clerical induction should be invested in the new commissary and after dinner, as the three men left together, Seymour claimed that Bray and Huitson had planned the whole affair. He swore that if Bray had not been wearing a gown "he would have satisfaction on him with his sword."[21] The governor was, perhaps, understandably angry at this attempted attack on his pocketbook, since the rights of probate of wills and induction of the clergy had belonged to the governors from the time of Lord Baltimore.

At any rate Bray did resign the office, no doubt weary after his years of fighting for the colony. He said, simply, "as for me, I have fought my fight; I have finished my course."[22]

In 1706 the living of St. Botolph's was offered to Bray again on the resignation of his friend, White Kennet, and this time he accepted the position, which he held for the rest of his life. While at St. Botolph's he continued working with the societies for a time, but when he was assured that they were going ahead with his plans, he gradually withdrew from active participation in their affairs; they continued, however, to call upon him throughout the remaining years of his life, for advice and assistance.

Literary Activities

In 1707, at the age of forty-nine, he completed the first—and only— volume of the greatly expanded second edition of *Bibliotheca Parochialis*. The list of books and annotations included in the volume were increased to over 400 pages, and yet they treated only two-thirds of the subjects outlined in the analytical table of contents. In the same year, he published a new edition of catechetical lectures, and devoted a large portion of his time to the religious education of the youth in his parish. He was asked to preach the annual sermon to the Society for the Reformation of Manners at St. Mary le Bow in 1708, which was later published under the title *For God or for Satan*.[23] In the following year, a funeral sermon preached at St. Clement's Danes was published as *The Good Fight of Faith*.[24]

The more than sixty libraries founded by Bray and the S.P.C.K. in England and Wales were given the protection of the Crown in 1709 through the help of Bray's friend, Sir Peter King, recorder of the City of London, who was successful in securing the passage of an act of Parliament "for the better Preservation of Parochial Libraries in that part of Great Britain called England."[25] Although the act has remained in force to the present day, little was ever done to enforce it throughout the years.

Bray was taken with a serious illness in 1723, and a group of his friends formed a voluntary society to assist him in his work. These Associates of Dr. Bray, as they were called, in addition to furthering his library plans, proposed to found schools for Indians and Negroes in the colonies. Bray recovered from his illness, and with the assistance of the Society for the Propagation of the Gospel he was able to send questionnaires to all of the missionaries in America in 1724, asking about the conditions of the libraries he had sent over. Though some of the libraries had been lost or neglected, he was gratified to learn that more than fifty of them were still in service.[26]

The writings of his later life, with one or two exceptions, show hasty and careless composition, and add little to his library plans. Rather, they testify to the loss of enthusiasm and zeal which characterized the books of his youth. In 1726, he returned to the study of libraries and missions once more, publishing his *Primordia Bibliothecaria*, a plan for developing parochial libraries ranging from an initial collection costing one pound, to a complete library costing one hundred. In *Directorium Missionarium*, published in the same year, he assembled a collection of materials about missions to Indians and Negroes. In 1727 he put together a rather hasty collection of books and tracts published under the title *Missionalia*, which contains a memorial attacking Bishop Berkeley's plans for a college in Bermuda.[27] He demonstrated the impracticality of the scheme, noting that Bermuda was not the magic isle invisioned by Berkeley, but a hard and barren land of poverty. He pointed out that the natives, if persuaded to enter a school, would quickly become so denationalized that their tribes would not take them back. It was better that missionaries, teachers, and craftsmen settle among them and show by example the virtues and advantages of civilization and Christianity, he felt.

Bray spent the final two years of his life writing the biographies of two obscure clergymen, Bernard Gilpin and John Rawlet, to illustrate the devotion of poor parish priests. In 1730 he published an edition of Erasmus's *Ecclesiastes*, which he considered to be one of the major influences in his life; he felt the separate edition was needed to set the work apart from the collected works of the author. At Bray's death the copyright for this work, along with Blair's *Discourses on the Sermon on the Mount*, were presented to the Associates, and they in turn were directed to present copies of the Erasmus to all young men of Oxford and Cambridge who were planning ordination. The book appears in the catalogs of nearly all of the libraries established by the Associates in England and America after Bray's death.

When Bray again fell seriously ill, in 1729, he had a feoffment drawn in his will empowering the Associates to administer the funds he had collected; later, as the "Associates of the Late Reverend Dr. Bray," they were given a charter by a decree in chancery.

On February 15, 1730, Bray died, and was buried in the churchyard of St. Botolph's, Aldgate. In his will he left most of the books he had collected to the Associates with the understanding that some were to be used to found libraries at Coleshill, Sheldon, and Ledsham. His personal library was to be presented to any town which could raise £50 for its support and establish a lending library. Maidstone was the recipient of the collection, and from an 1839 account of the library it then consisted of some 800 volumes, although many of them were in bad repair. Among those books remaining was a folio manuscript Bible, of which many of the leaves had been mutilated and from which all the illuminations had been cut out.[28] In 1961 the library that Bray presented to Sheldon, amounting to 360 volumes at that date, was deposited in the Reference Library of the Birmingham Public Library by the present rector of Sheldon, the Reverend D. J. Strickland, M.A.[29]

Bray lived a long and full life, continuing his enthusiasm to the end. In numerous villages and market towns throughout England and Wales, the remains of some 200 libraries founded by Bray and his Associates are presently being identified and cataloged under the direction of a committee set up by the Church of England. In America, only scattered volumes remain of Bray's attempt to found the first colony-wide library system. Perhaps they too can eventually be collected and preserved as a permanent tribute to this man, who valued the spiritual and intellectual well-being of his fellowmen far above his own material comforts. Few men have done more, and few have received less compensation for their pains, than Doctor Thomas Bray, Commissary of the Bishop of London to Maryland.

Chapter 3
The Design

Since 1634, when Archbishop Laud first claimed jurisdiction over the colonial congregations of the Church of England for the Bishop of London, little had been done to strengthen the position of the Church in America until the appointment of Henry Compton as Bishop of London in 1675. By then, the Civil War years and the Puritan government had nearly broken all contact between the Bishop and his American clergy. Compton, recognizing the weak position of the Church in relation to other denominations, quickly began to correct its deficiencies.

It was apparent to Compton that the Anglican colonists were in imminent danger of falling into spiritual neglect. Of the American colonies, New England was dominated by the Dissenters, Pennsylvania and the Jerseys by the Quakers, New York was largely Dutch, and Maryland had been ceded to the Roman Catholic Lord Baltimore. Only in Virginia and the Carolinas did the Church of England have some measure of establishment. Compton was able to secure a bounty of £20 from the king to be paid to those ministers agreeing to go to America. Although small, this inducement enabled the Bishop to interest several young clergymen in going to the plantations. In 1685, he sent the Reverend James Blair to Virginia, and four years later he appointed him his commissary for that colony.

Maryland was taken over by the Crown in 1691, at which time Governor Copley and the Assembly voted to create twenty-five parishes out of the ten counties of the colony, and endowed each with a maintenance requiring each taxpayer to contribute forty pounds of tobacco annually for the support of Anglican ministers. The Act of Establishment was revised and enacted in 1694, and was held to be in force until disallowed by the Crown. The two offending clauses causing the problems were: (1) The bill declared all of the laws of England in force in the colony, and (2) it

17

did not allow toleration for Dissenters. Governor Nicholson, in revising the act in 1694, requested that the Bishop of London appoint a commissary, for whom the Assembly promised a salary of £400 by assigning to him the rights of induction and probate, which belonged to the bishops in England but was vested in the governors in America. Compton's choice fell on Thomas Bray, who was offered the position in late 1695.

From the time of his appointment, Bray worked hard on the two problems he considered of utmost importance if the Church was to be secure in the colonies: the selection of missionaries and the establishment of libraries for them. Before his own trip in 1700, he had sent over several representatives to Maryland and to other colonies. The Reverend Thomas Clayton went to Philadelphia, and the Reverend Marshall to Charlestown, South Carolina; both took libraries with them. Although both men died within two years of their arrival, they managed to increase the congregations in their respective towns to over 700 communicants, and caused churches to be built.[1]

Bray's *Proposals*

Bray wrote to the Maryland Assembly in late 1695, suggesting that they revise and reenact the Act of Establishment by removing the offending clauses, while he continued to supply clergymen for their empty parishes. He immediately encountered difficulty, however, as it was exceedingly risky, even for men whose chances for success in England were slight, to settle in a distant land with uncertain prospects of salary, poor living conditions, and lack of any authority save for a bishop across the Atlantic. Only poorer men were likely to accept such a challenge, and to do their duty well, they needed books, which they were unable to purchase for themselves. Bray reasoned that if his clergymen could not afford books, their libraries had to be provided from another source, and so drew up a statement and presented it to the Bishop of London.

Compton immediately agreed to Bray's *Proposals* and presented them to his fellow bishops for approval; they were first printed in 1695 in "Small pica half sheets," and reprinted several times through 1700.[2] The bishops expressed their readiness to "contribute cheerfully towards these Parochial Libraries" and added the hope that "many pious persons, out of love for religion and learning" would do the same.[3] The proposals, as accepted by the higher clergy, were the first printed outlines of Thomas Bray's library plan, and show a remarkably clear grasp of the library problem, while simultaneously offering a rational solution for it.

In the pamphlet Bray began by lamenting the lack of books in the plantations, and pointing out how few of the clergy could afford to provide libraries of their own. Since a minister could do his best only if he had ready access to a library, Bray outlined a method that would endow each minister going to America with a "sufficient Library of well-chosen books" if his design was supported.[4] The main body of the paper consisted of two parts: the first was concerned with the type of books to be included in the libraries, and offered means of preserving and protecting them as well; the second outlined ways to acquire the books. It is interesting to note that eventually all of the suggestions Bray set forth in his proposals came back to him for implementation.

In Article 1, Bray suggested that a catalog be made of those books judged "most immediately and necessarily useful" for a minister to better "inform himself and instruct others." The Bishop of London could then send libraries composed of such books to each of the parishes in Maryland. The final catalog, when it appeared, was written by Bray himself.[5]

Article 2 was concerned with the preservation of the libraries for succeeding generations "without loss (as far as can be Humanly provided in any thing of that kind)." An exact catalog of all books was to be made for each parish library, with four copies to be recorded in books of vellum provided for that purpose. The first copy was to be left with the Bishop of London, the second with the commissary, the third was to remain in the library, and the fourth was to go to the vestrymen, the acting parish library board.

Article 3 made each minister responsible for his library and enjoined him to prevent loss of the books.

Article 4 stated that the commissary was to make a visitation once every three years to inspect all of the parochial libraries and see that no book was "imbezzel'd or lost." The church warden of each parish was required to inspect the library yearly and report its condition at the visitation.

Several writers have expressed doubts that Bray founded some of the libraries attributed to him because the books were stamped with the king's name on their covers. Article 5 stipulated that all books should carry the name of King William III on the front cover, and the name of the parish to which it belonged on the back.[6]

The final article provided for an Act of Assembly in each of the provinces, in effect making the minister responsible for those books lost through his own carelessness.

The second part of the *Proposals*, as previously mentioned, dealt with the means of acquiring books needed for the libraries, and the entries in Bray's accounts indicate his success in raising the necessary funds. He recommended that first the principal nobility, clergy, and gentry should be approached for contributions to "so pious a work." Merchants and traders who made their living from the colonies should be especially anxious to contribute, for "the more liberally they have reaped of their temporal things, the more they should sow to them in spiritual things." Application should also be made to "such Learned Authors as are now living," requesting the gift of some of their books judged useful.

With the support of the higher clergy, Bray had little difficulty in raising money and gathering books for the libraries. In addition he interviewed missionaries, solicited funds, planned a society to assist him in his work, and spent long hours at the Board of Trade and Parliament in fruitless efforts to secure passage of the Act of Establishment. He simultaneously continued writing and elaborating his library plans and his projected series on the catechism.

Bibliotheca Parochialis

In 1697 he published the bibliography he had suggested in the first article of his *Proposals*, the *Bibliotheca Parochialis*, containing a list of those books he thought necessary for a learned clergyman to be familiar with. Bray believed that to understand and preach the genuine doctrine of Christianity at least on a par with the "ordinary Laik [Laity]," the clergyman had to be provided with books. The lists following his introduction would cause any missionary to pause and seriously reflect before undertaking the hazardous voyage to the colonies, since the titles filled over 100 pages, and were greatly expanded in the second edition. The bibliography covered all fields of knowledge, complete with Bray's notes, generally in Latin, which summarized the books and emphasized their importance. Literally thousands of titles are included; the book affords both a precise indication of Bray's scholarship and an outline of ecclesiastical learning in the seventeenth century. Scattered throughout the notes are admonitions and bibliographical criticism, since Bray believed that in addition to a knowledge of theology, the clergy should have a well-rounded education, including natural history, mathematics, history, government, and law.

His original plan, as stated in the preface, was to publish a second volume which would contain civil, literary, personal, topographical, secret, fabulous, and miscellaneous history; biography; geography; voyages and travels; chronology; history of learning and the arts; universities; academies; libraries; and books. In looking through the table of contents for the proposed second volume, it is readily apparent why it never appeared, as sufficient material is outlined for a veritable encyclopedia of knowledge. Though he stated that the second volume was "well in hand" in 1697, no trace of it remains among his papers given to Sion College.

Apostolick Charity

About this time, he began to receive objections from the English clergy that he was neglecting them in favor of the colonies. Thus Bray immediately expanded his plans to include libraries for England and Wales, and published the most elaborate of his library statements up to that time.[7] In addition to supplying libraries for all poor ministers at home, he promised that, rather than libraries for Maryland alone, he would extend his endeavors and supply *all* of the English colonies in America. Furthermore, he was willing to visit each American colony and establish a library there personally.

Bray's *Essay* is by far the most complete statement of his library scheme for the colonies, but the exact type of library he envisaged is not clearly defined. The only published statement concerning the library service Dr. Bray intended to provide is found in the preface to *Apostolick Charity*, where he outlined three specific types of libraries for America. First was the parochial library, belonging to the minister and necessary for him to fulfill his functions. Second, he described the general or provincial library, "a Library of more Universal Knowledge" to be located in the chief town of each province for the use of all who wished "to launch out farther in the pursuit of Useful Knowledge, as well Natural as Divine." (See appendix A, table 1.) The last type, the layman's or lending library, was to be a collection of books furnished to the ministers and kept in the vestry for loan to the members of the parish. This collection would include a number of Bibles, catechisms, Common Prayer Books, and practical and devotional works to be loaned or given free, "especially in poorer Families." In addition to these three types of libraries, he felt it would be necessary to have free schools erected in each county, with at least one school in each province providing for the education of a half-dozen Indians, who could then return to their own people to civilize and convert them. All three types of libraries were sent to America, but the founding of schools had to await the establishment of the Society for the Propagation of the Gospel in Foreign Parts in 1701, save for the one school already established in Philadelphia by 1698.[8]

The preface to *Apostolick Charity*, entitled "A General View of the English Colonies in America with Respect to Religion," was compiled by Bray from surveys taken among those familiar with the colonies and from the results of his own efforts in sending missionaries and libraries to America. On publication of the book in 1699, Bray reported that libraries had been established in seven of the colonies in North America. In addition, two libraries had been sent to Jamaica, three to the Bermudas, one to St. Christopher's, one to Antigua, and one to Nevis. Of the twenty-one libraries then in existence in America, sixteen were in Maryland with one each in Boston, New York, Amboy, Philadelphia, and Charlestown. There were also sixty-one ministers and one schoolmaster at work in the colonies.[9]

Attached to a memorial of Bray's, published in 1700, were two interesting suggestions which indicate his desire to facilitate the dissemination of reading matter and improve and add to the libraries already established in America.[10] Had these suggestions been followed, the libraries he established might have lasted longer; from later developments in the library field, it is obvious that he was a century or more ahead of his time. His first suggestion required that libraries communicate reciprocal catalogs of their holdings in order "to lend what one may be provided with different from the other." The second, that a small annual subscription be provided by interested persons, with the books so purchased subsequently available to the subscribers to be "divided and shared by lot among them," later became a part of the subscription library movement of the eighteenth century, helping to "facilitate the procuring of new Books."[11]

After 1700 there was little further development of Bray's published library plans, although he continued his interest in the libraries for the rest of his life and tried repeatedly to secure their continuing existence. Among the Sion College manuscripts is another library work Bray left unfinished. Evidence indicates that it was written in 1701, for it includes nineteen catalogs of libraries he sent to America, the last dated 1701. The manuscript was entitled *Bibliotheca Americana Quatripartitae, or, Catalogues of the Libraries Sent to the Several Provinces of America Belonging to the Crown of England*.[12] The work is incomplete, with several roughly sketched parts forming a long preface which purports to show "the structure of these several Libraries and how far advanced towards their Perfection." As he related in the subtitle, Bray planned four types of libraries under the revised scheme: three were similar to the libraries in his earlier plans, while the fourth was to be the *Bibliotheca Decanalis*, a lending library for the clergy. He intended to divide each province into deaneries, each composed of five parishes, as in England. The library was to be lodged in the home of the chief clergyman of each deanery, and in addition to those books in the parochial library, it was to contain "some of the Primitive Fathers, as also a more enlarg'd list in Morality and History, not to speak of Grammars, Lexicons, and books in Rhetorick, Poetry and Logick." Bray finally had to abandon this idea when he found the rural deanery plan unfeasible in Maryland, where distances were greater than in England.

Since he personally established the foundations of a library system in America, there is little doubt that had Bray returned as commissary, his interest in the colonial libraries would have kept them alive. Unhampered by the numerous other projects which demanded his energies in England, he would doubtless have developed a flourishing system of libraries in Maryland, and perhaps established the chain of libraries down the Atlantic Coast from Newfoundland to Bermuda that he wrote of. If the flourishing religious societies in England had supplied him with books, funds, and the time to return to America, his surprisingly modern ideas might have led to an American public library movement in the eighteenth century. Because Bray could not return, however, his beloved libraries were forced to struggle on alone, depending on occasional benevolence from England for their very existence, with expansion and reciprocal communication existing only within the pages of his books.

Chapter 4
Financing the Design

Dr. Bray began raising the money needed to implement his plans as soon as the higher clergy approved his library scheme in 1695. His Accounts, which he presented for audit to the Society for the Promotion of Christian Knowledge in 1701, and to the Society for the Propagation of the Gospel in 1702 and 1704, indicate that he was indeed successful in his attempts. In the first volume of the Accounts, he listed in minute detail all of the contributions he received, from whom they came, and how they were expended.[1] The total of contributions received during the first period of solicitation amounted to £2,483.15.0, but during the same time Bray spent £2,958.13.4, leaving him an unpaid balance of £474.18.4. The money was spent for library books, tracts, and practical books for free distribution, the preparation of the books for shipment, and for the stamping of identifying symbols of ownership on the covers in gold, an expense in itself of £102.19.0.

Bray found that the King's Bounty covered the cost of the minister's passage to America, and the Assemblies guaranteed salaries for those clergymen emigrating to the colonies with some measure of establishment. In the other colonies, salaries were paid either with a grant from the Crown or through subscriptions raised in England. Bray felt some type of public support had to be secured to continue his projects, and he made repeated attempts to do so.

On March 3, 1698, a petition of Thomas Bray, D.D., was presented to the House of Commons concerning the bill then before it "for the better discovery of estates given to superstitious uses," asking that some of the proceeds recovered from those estates be directed towards the establishment of schools and libraries in America. The petition was referred to a committee for action, but the bill itself failed to pass.[2]

In the same year, following a ruling by Parliament that private parties could bid for the right to recover for themselves arrears in taxes due the Crown, Bray petitioned for the right to settle a dispute between the city of London and the Crown over ownership of a parcel of land in Old Street, London. There was £10 due in rent, and some small arrears in taxes. In the end, after expending £18 in drawing the petition and searching the deeds, Bray had to withdraw from the case with the ownership still in doubt.[3] Again, on February 15, 1699, he presented a petition to the surveyor general of Crown Lands, asking the Crown to grant him the rent and arrears of a parcel of land in Middlesex to be used to provide libraries for every parish in Maryland. The Treasury requested that the surveyor general report to the king on the rights and title to the land, but the records do not show any further action taken on the matter.[4]

The next attempt under the same bill occured on September 8 of the same year, when he petitioned the Crown for a grant of two-thirds of the debt of £1700 due from the firm of Francis Hollingshed and William Adderley. The petition also stated that Thomas Bray had "provided thirty Libraries in America to the value of £2,000, and was many hundreds of pounds out of purse already," and was seeking further assistence "to perfect the design." The petition was referred to the agent of taxes for study.[5] On December 10, 1700, after Bray had returned from Maryland, a Royal Warrant was sent to the clerk of the signet for a Privy Seal, which would grant two-thirds of the amount due to the Crown to Thomas Bray to reimburse him for his expenditures. His success in this affair was minor, however, for he had still not collected the money by April 3, 1703, when he received a petition from a certain William Lowndes requesting him to answer to the case of Samuel Adderley and "divers other purchasers of the lands of William Adderley deceased."[6] Lowndes was successful in his petition; Bray's Accounts indicate that he received only £150 from the estate, and it cost him £83.7.6 in procuring the grant. Although this was small return on his labor, the petition did prove fortunate in another way. While traveling to Holland to secure personally the king's signature on the Grant of Privy Seal, Bray met Abel Tassin, Sieur D'Allone, the king's secretary, who became deeply interested in Bray's plans, especially those concerned with conversion and education of the Negroes in the colonies. He gave Bray a small sum of money and promised more when his arrears in pension came to him; at his death in 1723, D'Allone bequeathed him £900 to aid in his work with the Negroes.[7]

During these years of struggle for public assistance, Bray's friend Governor Nicholson was attempting to ensure some means of support for the plan from the Maryland Assembly. On September 23, 1696, the Assembly resolved "to send a present to Dr. Bray for his endeavours to collect libraries."[8] On September 30, after Nicholson's repeated attempts to persuade the House of Burgesses to reimburse Bray for his expense in raising libraries for the colony, "the House, having refused a present to Mr. Bray is asked whether it expects people to do their business for nothing." The House continued to be stubborn, but finally, on May 31, 1697, they put an end to the quarrel with the following resolution: "As to the rewarding and reimbursing Mr. Bray for his trouble and expense concerning the libraries, resolved that a letter be written to him."[9] On November 7, 1698, Governor Nicholson granted the money arising from marriage licenses "if the marriage bill pass" to Dr. Bray "for his good service in collecting libraries." The bill did pass, and the House granted him £100 in 1699.[10] In the same year, in a letter to the Council of Trade and Plantations, Nicholson reported that "£100 had been given towards buying public libraries for the parishes."[11]

After Bray's visit to Maryland, when he met the members of the House in person, his chances of financial success at their hands were improved, and on May 7, 1700, "a present of £50 was made to Dr. Bray for as much as he has been very serviceable to this country in collecting libraries, etc." They followed this gift with another £50 on March 24, 1702, to help defray his expenses in fighting for the passage of the Act of Establishment.[12]

After his return from Maryland, Bray continued to receive gifts from several friends among the higher clergy, but attempt after attempt to achieve public support failed, while the problem of securing adequate funds continued. He returned to plans for a chartered society, which could accept bequests, invest money, and administer funds for special purposes. The failure of his first attempt in 1699 led to the formation of the voluntary Society for the Promotion of Christian Knowledge, and within this group Bray and four friends set up a special committee to collect money for the libraries. In addition to Bray, the group consisted of Francis, Lord Guilford, son of Lord North, Sir Humphrey Mackworth, Colonel Maynard Colchester, and Justice Hooke. The purpose of the committee, according to the first secretary of the S.P.C.K., John Chamberlayne, as set forth in a letter to Francis Nicholson, "is to assist Dr. Bray in raising libraries and in distributing practical books among the laity."[13] In his first report to the committee, Bray could state that "£2,000 had been spent on Libraries— Thirty well advanced and Seventy more a foundation laid."[14]

Bray submitted his accounts to the Society in June, 1701, showing that he had dispersed £631 more than he had received. The Society tried to repay him by charging a fee for membership admission and by requesting an annual subscription from members for founding schools and providing libraries and literature at home. The Society then decided to pay him five percent interest on the amount owed until such time as they could pay off the debt. On June 30, 1701, they promised to present him with all of the entrance subscriptions from new members until the sum was paid. On November 4, 1701, they ordered that "the share in the Mining Adventure be sold for £200," and on the 28th, Bray was paid in full.[15] Humphrey Mackworth was a founding member of the Society, and most of the members bought shares in his mining scheme. In 1701, they voted to donate one share of stock "towards promoting Libraries in North America," and gave one share to Bray personally.

Bray continued to receive a great number of private donations. His friend Robert Nelson bought a number of sermons to stock the libraries, and Sir Thomas Tynne, first Viscount Weymouth, continued to aid him with financial donations, as did the Society. Between July 1, 1701, and June 18, 1702, there are four entries in the *Minutes* regarding payments to Dr. Bray.[16] The references ceased from that date, as the S.P.C.K. turned its efforts to improve the literary lot of the poor clergy in England and Wales. Despite the hearty support Bray received from the Society and from friends all over England, the burst of enthusiasm which in 1697 had prompted him to attempt to "extend my endeavours for the supply of [libraries to] all the English Colonies in America" doubtless waned through these trying financial years, but he did not cease in his efforts.

After the formation of the Society for the Propagation of the Gospel in Foreign Parts in 1701, the S.P.C.K. withdrew from active participation in the foreign field. On October 28, 1701, it was resolved that "Subscriptions for the Plantations shall henceforth cease."[17]

The second accounting of funds was made to the S.P.G. on March 6, 1702, and indicated that from 1700, when Bray returned from Maryland, he had collected £1,624.15.6 and had expended £1,616.1.11, leaving him with a balance of £9.13.7. On March 25, 1704, he presented another statement of expenses to the S.P.G. covering the two-year period from the last audit, indicating that he had collected £943.3.0 and expended £967.1.7. The auditors noted that since the first audit in March, 1702, the balance due Dr. Bray had risen to £163.19.8.[18] From his accounts submitted to the societies, Bray had apparently expended over £5,000 on his library plans, both in England and America, from the time when he first accepted the position as commissary in 1695 until the last audit in 1704, quite an accomplishment at a time in which money was very scarce.

In 1704, Bray temporarily returned to Sheldon, a move which marked the end of his active participation in the societies he had been so instrumental in founding. He retained a large book collection at the time of his move, and gave it to the S.P.G. in the same year.[19] He continued to receive many gifts and donations for the libraries, and administered many of

27

them himself. At his death in 1730, he left the Associates a great store of books which they distributed; the catalogs of libraries sent out by the Associates contain a complete inventory of them.

Of more importance than the detailed records of the money raised and spent during the period are those parts of the Accounts indicating where the money went, which will be treated in the chapters devoted to the "Thirty [libraries] well advanced and Seventy more a foundation laid" Thomas Bray established in America.

Chapter 5
Securing the Design

Before he had sent out the first volumes for the libraries in 1696, Bray had been concerned for the protection of the precious books from "loss and embezelment." He had the covers stamped with signs of ownership and made elaborate plans to protect the books. Several approaches were open to him, and he explored them all, one after another.

As commissary, he hoped to visit each of the libraries personally every three years and inspect their condition. During the period between visitations, the members of the vestry were to inspect them periodically and report their findings to him. When events made it impossible for him to return to Maryland, he appointed a representative to serve as inspector of the libraries, and on June 30, 1700, he paid £10 to the Reverend Mr. Hall of Herring Creek, Maryland, to visit the libraries and report back to him.[1] This report, together with the inspection he had made himself when in Maryland, convinced him that someone in the colonies had to maintain strict supervision over the libraries if their existence was to continue. In a letter written to Speaker Smithson of the Maryland Assembly, who had been instrumental in the passage of the Act of Establishment, Bray pleaded for his support in convincing the ministers to send him catalogs of the libraries as he had requested many times, without success.[2]

A second avenue of approach was through the office of a resident bishop in the colonies who could oversee the clergy, schools, and libraries in America. Two functions essential to the spiritual life of the Church, confirmation and ordination, could only be exercised by a bishop under the Anglican constitution. Thus no colonist could become a practicing minister of the Church of England in America unless he could afford the time and money for the dangerous trip to England for his ordination. In a letter from the clergy of New York to the secretary of the S.P.G. in May, 1766, the dangers of the trip to England were clearly spelled out: two ministers were drowned near the entrance to Delaware Bay as they were returning from England to work in the colonies, and the clergymen reported that at least one out of every five men who went to England for Holy Orders perished in the attempt.[3] Samuel Johnson reported the same figures several times to the Society. His own son perished in England from smallpox while awaiting ordination. The lack of a bishop inhibited any systematic attempt at furnishing a liberally educated clergy within the limits of the colonies, and in the end, this lack converted the clergy of the Church of England into an alien class, standing outside the organic community life of the colonies.

Movements for a colonial bishopric began early in the eighteenth century. In 1702, John Talbot of Burlington, New Jersey, addressed a letter to the Bishop of London stating that there were "earnest addresses" from the colonists for a suffragan bishop. This letter was supported by a collective memorial from the clergy of New Jersey.[4] In 1701, Bray had addressed a memorial on the subject to the queen, showing a need for a colonial episcopate.

In 1711, Archbishop Sharp of York and Atterbury, then Prolocutor of the Lower House of Convocation, discussed the question with several other ecclesiastics, but the Bishop of London, through accident or indifference, took no part in the proceedings and the matter was dropped.[5] In 1713, the same year that a house was purchased in Burlington as a residence for a bishop, the queen was again memorialized on the subject by the S.P.G., and her reply was such as to raise that body's hopes.[6]

All hopes for success were dashed, however, with the death of Queen Anne and the accession of the House of Hanover in 1714. The Society immediately memorialized the new king on the subject, but he refused to grant their request because he thought it was supported by his enemies, the Tories. Although continued attempts were made throughout the eighteenth century, success was achieved only after the Revolution. Bray felt confident that with the appointment of a bishop, provision would be made for inspection and protection of the libraries; with the failure of the plan to gain the king's favor, however, he turned to other possible solutions.

While seeking out men to go to the plantations as missionaries in 1700, Bray decided to designate one of the ministers to oversee all of the libraries in the provinces. His friend White Kennett, struck with the idea, wrote to Thomas Hearne, then fresh out of Oxford, detailing the plan to him and suggesting that he discuss it with his patron, Mr. Cherry. If he accepted the position, he would be ordained at Bray's expense, have a library worth fifty pounds to take with him, and in addition receive a salary of seventy pounds per year, with an additional ten pounds for inspecting the libraries.[7] Cherry, in a letter to Hearne, referred to the matter and suggested that he decline the offer.[8] It was not until the appointment of George Keith as missionary of the S.P.G. in 1702 that a firsthand report on the condition of the libraries was made.

From the beginning another approach to the problem of security was available, and Bray had seized upon it immediately. Along with the catalogs sent to the colonies went a series of regulations for the management and protection of the libraries, based on his *Essay*. Using these rules as a guide, three of the colonial legislatures passed laws protecting and establishing the libraries as public libraries of the respective colonies. All of the laws are so similar in wording that the legislators undoubtedly used Bray's suggestions almost verbatim.

At least two laws concerning libraries were passed in Maryland before the South Carolina law of 1700, long considered to be the first law in America specifically pertaining to libraries. Unfortunately, Maryland's records prior to 1704 are missing due to a fire in the State House that year, and so it is impossible to point to any statute on the books earlier than 1704. Other sources indicate that when the law of 1704 was passed, two earlier laws had been in effect, the first dating from 1696, the second from 1698. On September 23, 1696, the House of Burgesses agreed that "a law be made to secure the Libraries that are to be bestowed upon the parishes." The next day, the Committee of Laws ordered that "a law should be made."[9] On October 2, "the House then attended the Governor and the following bills rec'd his assent.—Bill relating to the Commissary's Office, Bill for Parochial Libraries."[10] As further evidence of the law's passage, the Sion College manuscripts contain an abstract of the second law entitled "Library Law of the Province of Maryland, An.ii W. 1699, p.81." The law made the minister responsible for the protection of the library, provided for catalogs to be made for the use of the governor and vestry, and appointed Bray and his successors chief visitors to all the libraries in the province. Article 6 stated that a "Former act made 1696 for securing the Parochial Libraries repeal'd."[11] Bray's Accounts give further clues to the existence of such a law in the colony, for in 1698 Bray noted "46 paper books bound in vellum for Registers of Libraries . . . according to an Act of Assembly at 3s. per Book."[12]

Debates concerning the Charleston library appear in the records of the South Carolina Assembly as early as September, 1698, when the Assembly approved payment of "Fifty three pounds" to Mr. Clavell, London bookseller, for books for the library.[13] Further resolutions regarding letters of thanks to Bray and the Bishop of London, further payments for books, and a letter of thanks to the lords proprietors for their share in the library were also passed in 1698. On October 31, 1700, "a bill for securing the Provinciall Library in Charles Town in Carolina was read for the first time and past with amendments."[14] On November 7, "a Bill for securing the Provinciall Library in Charles Town in Carolina Read the Second Time and past with Amendments." It was ordered that William Smith, Esq., and Capt. Georg Raynor wait upon the governor with the bill.[15] Finally, on November 11, 1700, "a bill for Securing the Provincial Library of Charles Town in Carolina Read the Third Time and Past into Law."[16]

This act, as well as those from Maryland and North Carolina, contain striking similarities in text to the proposals for securing the libraries outlined in Bray's *Essay*. The bills could well have been prepared in England by Bray and sent, along with the libraries, as models for the colonial legislatures to follow. The South Carolina and Maryland laws differ from the law passed in North Carolina, in that the former placed the library in the hands of the rector of the Church of England. The North Carolina law provided for a library keeper to be elected by the commissioners. All the laws provided for the safekeeping of the books, made the library keeper responsible for the library, ordered catalogs made of the collections, provided for the appointment of a board of library commissioners with powers to sue at court in case of loss or damage, and outlined the rules for circulation. No fines were levied for overdue books, but the laws did provide for a charge of three times the value of the book in case of loss or damage. Terms of circulation varied, with four months for a folio, two months for a quarto, and one month for an octavo or smaller. All books were to be returned each year in order that the commissioners could inspect the collection. Section 8 of the South Carolina law named the library commissioners, and Section 9 ordered that the books be returned before January 1 so that a complete catalog could be made of them.[17]

The next legislation in point of time was the passage of the Maryland library act of 1704, which did not substantially differ from any of the other laws. The law passed in North Carolina in 1705 is notable in that it also provided for the establishment of the town of Bath, where the library had been sent.[18] Edward Moseley, the Speaker of the North Carolina Assembly, who was instrumental in securing passage of the act, had cataloged the Charleston library two years earlier.[19]

A supplementary act was passed by the South Carolina Assembly on June 7, 1712, when it was discovered that many books had been badly used. This act indicates that the library had been used, but also showed that the citizens of Charleston did not take the best of care of their public library. The new act stated that, since unrestricted use had "proved very prejudicial to the said library, several of the books being lost and others damnified," the Assembly found that it had to give discretionary powers to the library keeper, who could refuse to loan a book to anyone he thought would not care for it. The act also changed the date of the commissioners' meeting to the third Wednesday in March and the third Wednesday in October, making their inspection semiannual. It further provided for the election of additional commissioners and made them the visiting board for all of the libraries in the province.[20] A revision of the North Carolina act was passed in 1713, which stopped the rumors maintaining that the library had been largely destroyed in 1712.[21] Maryland had to pass a stronger law in 1714 to enforce earlier acts when Governor Hart discovered that many of the books were lost or stolen.

Despite the legislation and Bray's repeated attempts to find some means of protecting the libraries for future generations, the libraries did not long survive his own death. True, remnants of them existed long after the statutes had disappeared from the books, but without active interest they could not long survive neglect and loss. They suffered much the same fate as the English libraries, protected by the Parochial Library Act of 1709; however, they do show that the local authorities were interested in protecting them, without providing any financial support. Without the addition of new materials, any library soon ceases to hold the interest of its users; thus as the century advanced, Bray's great plan slowly faded from the consciousness of the colonists, until the remaining books were filed away in the archives, where many of them are today, silent moldering symbols of an idea in advance of its time.

Scanty though early Maryland records are, there is still proof that the vestrymen continued their duties in the inspection of the libraries well into the eighteenth century. In the vestry book of All Saints' Parish, Calvert County, it was recorded on December 3, 1734, that the vestry adjourned for one hour to meet at the house of the minister, Mr. James Williamson, to view the library. They found it all in order except for two books which were missing.[22] Theodore Gambrall, in his church history of Maryland, related many such visitations down to the time of the Revolution.[23]

Bray had the pleasure of founding the libraries and the gratification of knowing that some people cared enough about them to pass laws for their protection and preservation. His only regret was that no public means could be found to guarantee that they would grow and flourish for the use of future generations.

Chapter 6
The Provincial Library

From the fall of 1695, when he first became commissary, until late 1704 when he withdrew from active involvement in the religious societies, Bray succeeded in establishing and collecting books for five provincial libraries, thirty-eight parochial libraries, and thirty-seven layman's libraries in America. He contributed money to the College of William and Mary, financially helped lay the foundation for parochial libraries in all of the thirty parishes in Virginia, and provided small collections of books to be placed at Boston, New York, Philadelphia, Annapolis, and Williamsburg for the Reverend George Keith's work in converting the Quakers. During this same nine year period, Bray also found the time to establish six libraries in Newfoundland and several in the West Indies, and sent over 34,000 volumes to the colonies to be given away free for the layman's libraries.

The provincial libraries sent to Annapolis and Charleston were considered from the first to be the public libraries of the provinces. The legislatures of both provinces accepted them as such and attempted to give them legislative and financial support and continuity. The libraries sent to Boston, New York, and Philadelphia, on the other hand, were treated by the ministers as the property of the respective parishes, and it is doubtful that anyone outside of the Anglican community ever had free access to them. The library sent to Bath, North Carolina, in 1700, although considered a parochial library by Bray, was designated the public library of the province by the colonists who passed laws to protect it, and is today properly classified as the sixth provincial library established in America.

Since a complete history of the libraries established by Dr. Bray has not been written, there has been some confusion in historical writings as to their size, contents, and location. However, since catalogs of most of the libraries survive, and since Bray's own Accounts give the number and location of the libraries he established, it is possible to sketch the history of the more important collections while simultaneously clearing up some of the confusion that still exists.

Annapolis

Bray's first concern, understandably, was for the colony over which he had been appointed commissary, and so his greatest efforts were expended in providing for the spiritual and intellectual welfare of Maryland. The first libraries were sent there, among them the provincial library at Annapolis in honor of Princess Anne of Denmark, for whom the new capitol had been named. This library, containing 1,095 volumes, was the largest single collection sent to America by Thomas Bray. The thirty parochial libraries sent to Maryland ranged in size from 10 to 314 volumes, and in all over 2,500 volumes and 6,000 tracts were sent to that colony before 1700.

The Assembly and the governor looked upon these libraries as part of a colony-wide library system from the time they first arrived. Since the library at Annapolis was the largest in the system, it naturally received the greatest share of attention from the colony's lawmaking body. Unfortunately this "premier Library" is the only library established by Bray for which no original catalog exists. Catalogs of the provincial libraries sent to Boston, New York, Philadelphia, and Charleston show that approximately two-thirds of the volumes were religious or theological works, and the remaining one-third was composed of what Bray referred to as "Human Knowledge," which included history, geography, medicine, philosophy, and poetry. Since books still remaining from the Annapolis collection show roughly this same percentage of nonreligious works, it can be assumed that the proportion was nearly the same in the original library.

The earliest existing description of the contents of the Annapolis provincial library is recorded in a catalog of St. John's College, made in 1847. This catalog listed 442 volumes under the heading "Ancient Classics and Divinity." Included were volumes by Ambrose, Athanasius, Augustine, Pearson on the Creed, Burnett on the Articles, Sherlock on Death, and many other works by the church fathers and seventeenth-century divines, as well as titles by Virgil, Plutarch, Euripides, Aristophanes, Claudius, Curtius, Horace, Livy, Martial, Ovid, and Plautus.

By 1966, the collection numbered 211 volumes of the original 1,095, kept in an alcove of the library of St. John's College. The books were all stamped on the front cover with the words: *Sub Auspiciis Wilhelmi III*, and on the back with the words: *De Bibliotheca Annapolitana*. Remnants of the library also include Boyle's *Works*, volumes by Henry More, Bishop Burnett's *History of his Own Time*, and volumes by Grotius and Puffendorf. The medical books remaining include Ludovico de la Forge, *Tractatus de mente humana*, Richardo Lower's *Tractatus de corde*, and several other works of this kind. In the field of popular literature, the novel is represented by John Barclay's *Argenis* in Latin, a book found in several other Bray libraries.

From a comparison with the other provincial library catalogs, none of which approached this one in size, it is probable that the original collection contained numerous other nonreligious works. Of the three volumes of poetry in the New York library, for instance, one was Milton's *Paradise Lost*, and it is possible that this work appeared in the library at Annapolis as well. Regardless of the contents of the total collection, however, it compared favorably with the only two other nonprivate colonial libraries, those of Harvard and William and Mary, both of which were destroyed by fire at an early date. Those early collections which escaped destruction by fire suffered as badly from poor care and inadequate supervision; thus the only books which have survived were those absorbed by other libraries. Interest in the Annapolis library faded after the first quarter of the eighteenth century, and when it was absorbed by St. John's College in 1786, few people were aware of its existence, much less its origin. Most library historians assumed that it had disappeared along with most of the smaller libraries by the time of the Revolution.

Historic tradition—without factual basis—has maintained that the library was kept in the commissary's office in the State House until that building burned in 1704, at which time the books were safely removed to King William's School.[1] From the surviving records, it is possible to follow the library from its arrival in 1696–97 until it was finally deposited at St. John's College in 1786. It is probably true that the library was first placed in the commissary's office on the second floor of the State House, above the porch, since in 1697 the Assembly voted that "the library should be placed in the office and under the care of the commissary of the province, permitting all persons desirous to study or read the books to have access thereto under proper restrictions."[2] In 1699, while the Assembly was in session, a fire broke out which destroyed part of the upper chambers before it was extinguished.[3] Because of the damage to the second floor, it was decided to move the library from the building. On May 1, 1700, the council debated on "some convenient place to secure the Public Library." On May 9, the Assembly agreed that the library be placed in the "free school in the room pitched upon untill such time as it can otherwise be disposed of."[4] It was ordered that Major Thomas Smith and Colonel John Thompson return to the governor and visitors of the Free School their thanks for their concurrence in ordering a room in the school for the library.

36

In the beginning, the school had offered the space free of charge, but on April 15, 1706, a petition from the rector of the school to the Assembly was presented asking for £72 for six years' rent.[5] The same petition claimed rent for "a Council Room" at King William's School for the same period, so it would seem the Assembly met there periodically during the early years of the eighteenth century.

Since the commissary was the chief overseer of the library, the original plans specified the removal of the library to his house when it was finished, but in all probability the library remained in the school until the property was taken over by St. John's College after the Revolution.[6]

The Annapolis library was the first library in America to receive official recommendation that public funds be applied to its maintenance. In 1697, Governor Nicholson proposed to the House of Burgesses that the king be requested to designate a portion of the funds furnished to buy arms for the colony to be set aside for the purchase of books for the "public library at Annapolis." He also asked that part of the public revenue be applied to the enlargement of the collection.[7] Had this proposal been carried out, it might have had far-reaching consequences in the development of public libraries in America, since it would have provided a firm foundation for the Annapolis library and might have served as an example for the other colonies to follow in providing for the increase of their own libraries. Unfortunately on September 24, 1697, the Committee on Laws reported that they thought the country was not yet sufficiently supplied with arms; when it was so supplied, they would be ready to address the king on the matter.[8]

Although the governor's suggestion failed to meet the approval of the House, that body did find it possible to supply money for the library at least once, as reported in Nicholson's letter to the Board of Trade on February 4, 1699, when he stated that "one hundred pounds has been given towards purchasing public libraries for the parishes."[9]

Since all of the library's early records have disappeared, no evidence remains that Bray ever added to the library as he did to others, but since this was admittedly his favorite library, he doubtless did add to it from time to time. Other Maryland libraries contained books published as late as 1729 and 1748 which are now on deposit in Maryland's diocesan library, the Wittingham Memorial Library, so it is possible that some books were added to the 1,095 originally sent to Annapolis in 1696 and 1697.

Bernard Steiner, writing of the libraries in Maryland at the end of the nineteenth century, called the Annapolis library the "most considerable public collection of books in British North America," and the first circulating library in the colonies.[10] As proof that the books did circulate, he reported that Governor Hart, on taking inventory in 1714, discovered that several books had not been returned. "On learning of this, the Assembly ordered the several sheriffs to publish notices commanding all persons having books from the Public Library to return them."[11]

Charleston

Of all the provincial libraries, Charleston's alone was a joint endeavor, with Bray, the Carolina Assembly, and the lords proprietors united in raising the money for the book collection. Bray's Accounts show that he raised £300 for Carolina, and bought 225 books with this sum. The first shipment of books arrived in 1698 in the care of the Reverend Samuel Marshall, newly appointed minister to Charleston.[12] On receipt of the books, the Assembly ordered on October 8, 1698, that Captain Howes and Mr. Izard write a letter to the Bishop of London and Dr. Bray and thank them for laying the foundation of a "good and Publick Library."[13]

The money from the lords proprietors seems to have arrived at the same time, as a letter was ordered written with "Thankes of this House for their Generous Present of soe Considerable Part of our Publick Library."[14] The Accounts for October 25, 1699, show that Bray sent a "Box with Books to Carolina." On August 16, 1701, Bray sent an additional collection to the library. The books arrived safely, for on January 31, 1702, Nicholas Trott reported that Dr. Bray had sent "Sundry Books as Addition to ye publick Library" as well as another "Collection of books for a Layman's Library." It was ordered that Trott write a letter to Dr. Bray thanking him for this additional gift.[15]

Library costs soon exceeded the original sum of £300, since the library room had to be fitted out with tables and shelves for which, on March 1, 1701, the House paid Mr. Chevalier Joyner the sum of fourteen dollars.[16] On September 10, 1701, the sum of "One pound and five shillings" was appropriated to pay for "freight and other Charges of Sundry Books given to this Country by Dr. Thomas Bray of London."[17] One additional amount was charged, to pay Edward Moseley "the Sume of two Pounds Tenn Shillings for transcribing the Catalogues of ye Library Books," on May 7, 1703.[18] By that date, Dr. Bray's third gift had reached the colony, containing additional books for the public library and further volumes and tracts for the layman's library.[19]

As he did for several of the other colonies, Governor Nicholson presented South Carolina with thirty guineas to buy books in 1705, and also contributed twenty pounds for support of ministers there.[20]

The Charleston library contained a surprisingly well-rounded collection for its time. Of the 225 original volumes, 83 were of a nonreligious nature. This number included 42 titles in history, voyages and travels, 15 in physiology, anatomy, surgery, and medicine, 6 in mathematics, 6 grammars, and 2 volumes of poetry. In the field of the humanities were such works as Roger L'Estrange's translation of Aesop's *Fables*, Plutarch's *Works* in five volumes, and the Delphine editions of Terence, Virgil, Horace, Juvenal, and Persius. The two volumes of poetry were Sothey's *Life of Christ* and an unidentified version of *King Arthur and his Knights*. A miscellaneous work listed in the catalog was the *Works* of King James in one folio volume. The religious and theological works included titles by most of the church fathers, commentaries and controversial works, and books by eminent seventeenth-century English theologians, as well as sermons by Beveridge, Bull, and Atterbury.

Precise information concerning the exact use made of the library is scanty, but some interesting observations were made in 1712 by Commissary Gideon Johnston, the S.P.G. missionary at Charleston, in his report to the secretary of that Society. He reported that over one-third of the library had been "imbezl'd" by his successors. He also objected to the library law which allowed free access for all to the collection, and the fact that the borrowers refused to return books in their possession.[21]

An attempt was made to remedy Johnston's complaints in the same year, when a supplementary act was passed restricting the use of the library to those approved by the library keeper as responsible borrowers. This was the last reference to the library until 1724, when the Reverend Thomas Morritt, recently appointed schoolmaster at the Free School in Charleston, reported that there were only "six Classic Authors" remaining in the collection, and no catalog of the library could be found.[22]

It is probable that, with each succeeding library keeper, more and more of the books were "imbezl'd" until 1724, when only the "six Classic Authors" remained. The library's losses became less of a serious problem to the clergy after this time, because they were supplied with books by the S.P.G., while the laymen of the community were able to purchase books from the newly established booksellers. In 1732, Edward Wigg advertised a large assortment of books imported from England which included histories, memoirs, novels, plays, and travels, as well as works in several other fields.[23]

Although the Charleston library met the needs of clergy and layman alike at the beginning of the eighteenth century, it suffered, as did the other provincial libraries, from the legislature's failure to offer it real protection and a guaranteed means of increase. Tied perhaps too closely to the Anglican church, it gradually decreased in size until it ceased serving the needs it was designed for, and the colonists turned to other sources for their reading material.

Bath

When Thomas Bray dispatched the Reverend Mr. Brett with his parochial library to St. Thomas Parish in "Pamplico, North Carolina" in 1700, the town of Bath did not exist. Most of the colony's population was centered around Queen Anne's Creek, now Edenton, and Albemarle, which was the largest metropolis of the colony at that time. Several attempts were made to have the library moved to Albemarle or Edenton without success. In 1705, Bath was "incorporated and made a Township" in the same act that created the public library, entitled: *An Act for Appointing a Town in the County of Bath; and for Securing the Publick Library Belonging to St. Thomas's Parish in Pamlicough.*[24] Bray considered the Bath Library a parochial library, although the North Carolina Assembly considered it the provincial library of the colony.

Despite attempts to move it, the library remained in the new town of Bath. In 1712 the historian Rainsford reported that the books had "all been dispersed and lost by those wretches that do not consider the benefit of so valuable a gift."[25] Two years later John Urmstone, an Anglican minister working in North Carolina, reported that "the famous library sent in by Dr. Bray's directions is, in great measure, destroyed. I am told the books are all unbound and have served for some time as waste paper."[26] Both of these statements are apparently misleading, in view of the trouble the Assembly took to revise the statutes of 1715, which included the library act, and to change the names of the library commissioners. The act was again reprinted in Swann's Revisal of 1752, and since Edward Moseley did most of the work on the revision he certainly would have dropped the act from the statutes as obsolete, as was done in 1765, when it was reported in the revision that "the books are mostly scattered and no library keeper appointed for many years."

Edward Moseley offered his library to the S.P.G. in 1723 to establish a library in Edenton. Some early historians claimed that this library was the remains of the Bath library, which had somehow fallen into his hands, but a comparison of the catalogs of the two libraries shows this to be false, with the Moseley collection more closely resembling those sent out by the Society for the Propagation of the Gospel to their missionaries. Whether the Bath library was eventually taken by Urmstone, who tried several times to remove it to Edenton, or whether it actually fell into a state of complete decay, is unknown; it must have been substantial enough in the eyes of the Assembly, however, since they revised an act for its protection for nearly fifty years.

The catalog of the Bath collection shows that it contained 166 volumes, with 109 in octavos, 19 in quartos, and 38 in folios. In addition to the theological works were 48 volumes of a nonreligious nature, which included 11 works on history and travel, 2 geographies, 5 dictionaries, 3 mathematics books, 3 natural history works, 3 on heraldry, 3 biographies, 3 law books, 4 classics, 4 grammars, 3 books of essays, 2 books on sports, and 1 each on medicine, mythology, and poetry.[27] Though this was the smallest collection sent to serve as the chief library for a province, the collection shows the same relative percentage of works in the various fields of knowledge as do the provincial libraries established in the other colonies, and probably would have successfully served the needs of the people from the beginning had it been located in the colony's population center, at either Edenton or Albemarle.

Boston

When Lord Bellomont arrived in May of 1698 to assume his new duties as royal governor of New York, he brought with him Bray's three libraries destined for Boston, New York, and Philadelphia. Francis Greenwood, after studying the catalog preserved in the church records of King's Chapel, called the collection "a theological library which was perhaps the best at that time in this country."[28] He related that the library was kept for a time in the house of the Reverend Miles, rector of the church; this was borne out by a letter written to the Bishop of London, thanking him for the library.[29] Mr. Miles paid three pounds on October 2, 1698, "for chests for the King's Library," and again in November he "paid for more chests, in all 12 boxes."[30]

The library was kept in the houses of the successive ministers of King's Chapel until the Revolution, when, like most of the colonial collections, it suffered some damage. In 1807 the remaining books were deposited in the Theological Library of First Church, which had been established shortly before. The First Church of Boston, founded in 1632, burned at the end of the eighteenth century. The new building, which opened in 1808, contained space for a theological library, and the books from King's Chapel were deposited there in the same year. A catalog of this library, published in 1808, listed the books from King's Chapel separately.[31]

Originally, the library contained 221 volumes. (See appendix B for a catalog of the collection.) Bray sent additions to the library in 1701, 1702, and 1704. The catalog preserved at King's Chapel listed 288 volumes; of these, 251 were deposited in the Theological Library in 1807, and between that date and 1823, 37 volumes disappeared. In 1823 it was voted that the Theological Library be placed in the Boston Athenaeum.[32] Josiah Quincey, in his history of the Athenaeum, reported in 1823 that "in the Summer of this year the library of King's Chapel and the Theological Library belonging to the Boston Association of Ministers, were deposited in the Athenaeum." He noted that the ministers of King's Chapel and the proprietors of the Theological Library were to be entitled to all the privileges of life subscribers to the Athenaeum, as long as their books remained in the library. Quincey went on to report that "these libraries made an addition of thirteen hundred volumes, some of them rare works."[33] The books from the two libraries were distributed, according to their subjects, throughout the collection. Those of the King's Chapel library at time of deposit amounted to 214 volumes; since that time only 6 have disappeared. In 1881, because of its value as a library exemplifying colonial culture, the King's Chapel collection was reassembled and placed in a special case purchased by the congregation of the church.[34] Today, 110 of the original volumes still bear the royal stamp on the cover, although most of the remainder have been rebound.

Because of the special efforts made in 1698 to secure the Church of England in Massachusetts, this library contained a greater number of theological works than any other provincial library. Only 25 volumes were of a nontheological nature, and they included 17 histories, 1 mathematics book, 2 grammars and lexicons, and 5 books in the humanities. Bray made 13 additions on August 14, 1701, including one set of 6 volumes in mathematics, and More's *Religious and Philosophical Works*, also in 6 volumes.[35] Even those volumes listed as history in the catalog were inclined to be religious in nature, save for Baker's *Chronicles of the Kings of England*, Dugdale's *Views of the Late Troubles*, and a copy of Varenius's *Geography* with Sanson's maps.[36]

Since King's Chapel remained for many years a lone Anglican outpost in Dissenter New England, the library in all probability was used only by the ministers and their congregations, and not made available to the general public. Today it remains as the third largest of the provincial library collections still in existence, with only those at Annapolis and Philadelphia being larger. The libraries sent to Bath and Charleston have entirely disappeared; only a handful of books from the New York library remain, and these are scattered in several collections.

New York

Trinity Church, which housed the provincial library of New York from 1698 to 1776, was opened in March of 1698. Governor Fletcher, who had arrived in 1693, asked the Assembly to provide for the maintenance of a minister of the Church of England for the city, as ordered in his instructions. The vestrymen appointed as the first minister William Vesey, a 1693 graduate of Harvard College and, according to Lord Bellomont, "the son of a Jacobite who had been pilloried at Boston for his adherence to the cause of the House of Stuart."[37] At the urging of the governor in 1697 Vesey went to England and took orders in the Church of England. After his return, he continued to serve as rector of the church for nearly fifty years.

The New York provincial library arrived with the new governor in 1698, as did those of Boston and Philadelphia. Under the heading "a Register of ye Books Sent Toward Laying ye Foundation of a Provincial Library in New York," Bray listed 157 titles numbering 220 volumes and costing

£ 70.[38] A duplicate of the catalog was copied into the Vestry Book of Trinity Church in 1698.[39] In the same year the retiring governor Fletcher presented a number of books to the library. Other evidence indicates that the books were kept in Trinity Church from their arrival: in a letter to Colonel Nicholson, Vesey wrote that "a happy society of several ministers of the city was maintained in the Church Library."[40] Other references to the library appear in the vestry records and show that it was augmented five times by Dr. Bray between 1701 and 1712, additions also confirmed by Bray's own accounts. On June 2, 1701, the vestry examined the library "according to the catalogue sent from Dr. Bray and signed the same returned with an account of what Books were wanting & were not as in the Catalogue."[41]

The New York collection was the smallest of the provincial libraries save for the one sent to Bath, North Carolina. Of the 220 volumes, 189 were theological works; among the remaining volumes, 6 were in the field of the humanities, 23 in history, voyages, and travels. Two were medical books, 6 were grammars and lexicons; finally, there was 1 rhetoric, 1 logic, and 3 volumes of poetry, these last listed as "Poetae Antiqui, Buchanani Psalmi, and Milton's Paradise Lost." Additions over the next fourteen years brought the collection up to 266 volumes. The last book listed among the additions was "the Earle of Clarendon's *History of the Rebellion,* 3 vols. fol." Other books sent during the same period included Gordon's *Geography Anatomiz'd,* a book of mathematics, Keith's *Narratives,* and several other anti-Quaker tracts, including Bugg's *Pilgrim's Progress from Quakerism to Christianity,* a large number of collected sermons, and several other religious works. The library also received donations from other sources; for instance, at a vestry meeting on June 13, 1707, Mr. Vesey reported that "Thomas Byerly Esquire has presented the public library with books amounting to six pounds which are put down in the Catalogue thereof."[42]

When George Keith, a Quaker convert, was sent to America in 1702 as the first of many missionaries sponsored by the Society for the Propagation of the Gospel in Foreign Parts, he carried instructions from Thomas Bray to inspect the libraries in his travels along the coast. In a letter to Bray written from Philadelphia in 1703, Keith reported that he had "view'd the Library at Boston, as ye ordered me, and find it in good condition. But at N. York I could not have the catalogue." He went on to report Mr. Vesey's statement that the "Chaplain of the Fort had carried it away with him to England."[43]

Because the Anglican congregation represented a minority group in New York, the library was unable to serve the interests of all of the people. In 1724, Mr. Vesey reported, in his reply to the questionnaire sent out by Dr. Bray and the S.P.G., that the books were "preserved and kept in good condition." There is little doubt that the collection had been well preserved: in fact the Reverend Robert Jenney, chaplain at the fort and assistant minister of Trinity Church, complained that the collection was inaccessible. The library was evidently kept locked in Mr. Vesey's study, following the 1698 instructions of the vestry.

Beginning in 1715, a number of additions to the library were made by Robert Elliston, who gave a collection of plate to the church, as well as books to the library. From 1715 until the last recorded gift in 1741, Elliston donated 116 volumes to the collection. The catalog of his gifts is entered directly after the Bray library in the vestry books of Trinity Church, where Mr. Elliston is identified as "General Comptroller of His Majesty's Customs in New York."[44] No further mention of the library is made in the church records until September 21, 1776, when the church building, the rectory, and the school were destroyed by fire. At that time, the value of the library, which was almost a total loss, was placed at £200.[45] In a long letter to the secretary of the S.P.G., the Reverend Charles Inglis, rector of the church (and eventually the first Bishop of Nova Scotia), related the trials and tribulations of the Anglican clergy during the Revolution, and described the fire which destroyed the church and caused the loss of over 1,000 homes, nearly one-fourth of the city.[46] Those few volumes which were saved were placed in St. Paul's Church for safe-keeping until the end of the war; they eventually found their way to the New York Historical Society Library and other libraries in the city.

Philadelphia

The Philadelphia Provincial Library was housed in Christ Church, which had been erected in 1695. The first authorized minister in the city was Thomas Clayton. He was called "the Minister of the Doctrine of Devils" by the Quakers because of his success in converting so many of their number to the Church of England.[47] Like George Keith, one of his specific missions was to convert the Friends, as Bray felt they were outside the Christian community. In order to combat, in his opinion, the insidious influence of Clayton and Keith, William Penn "sent 2 or 300 books against George Keith by R. Jenny, which may be disposed of as there is occasion and service."[48] Despite this effort and the constant Quakers' vigilance, Keith, Clayton, and later Evan Evans, Clayton's Welsh successor at Christ Church, were able to convert many of the younger Friends to the Church. Evans also preached at the churches of his fellow Welshmen at Chester, Chichester, Concord, Radnor, Montgomery, and Perkiomen. During his visits to those churches he gave out a great quantity of *The Whole Duty of Man, The Practice of Piety*, and many other religious tracts translated into Welsh by the Society for the Promotion of Christian Knowledge.[49]

According to the catalog in his Bibliotheca Provincialis Americanae, Bray dispatched 327 volumes to Philadelphia. Religion and theological works accounted for 210 volumes, and the remainder were distributed similarly to those in the other provincial library collections. The books were all stamped on the covers "For the Library of Philadelphia." In 1701, Bray sent an additional collection of 13 volumes to the library, and he followed this gift with others in 1702 and 1704. On May 2, 1718, the vestry ordered that an inventory of the library be taken because Mr. Evans was leaving the church for a living in Virginia.[50]

Since the original Christ Church building was quite small, the congregation soon outgrew it, and work was begun on a new brick church in 1727. The building was completed in 1744, and the library placed in a specially designed room in the church.

In 1728, a donation of 100 volumes bound in vellum was received from Ludovic Sprogell, a member of the parish. A number of people outside the church also donated books to the collection, among them Thomas Penn, Thomas Graeme, William Talbot, and the Bishop of Oxford. In 1730, it was reported that the library contained over "500 circulating volumes."[51] Several valuable books were donated to the library by the Reverend Archibald Cummings, rector of the church, in 1741. In 1753, Dr. Bearcroft, secretary of the S.P.G., wrote to the vestry and reported that the Reverend Charles Chambres had left £500 to the Society to be used to purchase books for the Christ Church library. With that sum, Bearcroft was able to buy 347 volumes, which were duly listed in the vestry book of the church.[52]

As other donations were made to the library, the collection grew steadily, and on August 18, 1766, the vestrymen ordered that a new catalog be made. The Reverend S. Preston gave a Polyglot Bible and several other books to the library in 1789; this proved to be the last addition to the library entered in the vestry books.[53]

Housed in a brick building from the first, the library of Christ Church was the only one of the provincial libraries which survived the ravages of fire, war, and pillage. It continued to be housed in the church until 1966, when the collection was deposited in the Library Company of Philadelphia. A description of the collection appears in the Annual Report of that library for 1966.

It is unfortunate that existing records do not show how heavily these provincial libraries were used by the people. The numerous letters of thanks preserved in the S.P.G. archives testify that they were appreciated. Such a group of libraries, amounting to 2,245 volumes in 1698, must have filled a great gap in the intellectual needs of those who had access to them. Literally hundreds of letters from missionaries throughout the eighteenth

45

century indicate the importance these men placed on the libraries; letters from ministers in the smaller towns decried the lack of reading materials, and most sent requests to the Society for the Propagation of the Gospel for books to add to their static collections.

The popularity of the libraries ended with the Revolutionary War. Fire, theft, and pillage by soldiers on both sides reduced the collections; in some instances, wanton destruction of the libraries occurred. Books which survived the war were neglected for many years, unless they found their way into the larger collections which still preserve them.

Too close an association with the Church of England doomed the libraries once the war came; and once it was over, ties with the home country were broken. Many members of the Anglican Clergy who had remained loyal to the Crown left the colonies for Canada or England when the Revolution was over, and several of them took the remainder of their libraries with them. American literature, then in its infancy, began to fill the void left by these now-dispersed collections; and, as they no longer filled a need of the people, the books were stored and forgotten until brought to light by design or serendipity over the past 200 years.

Chapter 7
Two Other Libraries

In addition to the provincial libraries, Bray sent two other types of collections to the colonies. The parochial library was intended to function as the personal library of the minister, and the layman's library was to be loaned or given outright to the colonists. Bray believed that books so given to the members of the congregations would strengthen their religious convictions, while books given to non-Anglicans might bring about their conversion to the Church of England.

The Parochial Library

Although the parochial library was designed for the minister's personal use, evidence exists indicating that the books in the libraries often circulated, and that the libraries also contained many books which were not entirely religious in nature. For example, the parochial library sent to Bath, North Carolina, was immediately adopted as the provincial library; the contents of the collection were described in the preceding chapter.

Many of the parochial libraries were in fact quite generalized in their contents. Such libraries were sent to Newport, Rhode Island; to St. James Parish, Anne Arundel County, Maryland; and to the parishes of St. Mary's and St. Paul's, also in Maryland. Often even the smallest of the libraries contained books of a nonreligious nature, since Thomas Bray believed that every minister should be familiar with all areas of knowledge. (For a list of the parochial libraries established by Thomas Bray, see appendix A, table 2.)

Fundamentally, the parochial library was designed to aid the preaching and catechizing minister in instructing his congregation in "all things necessary to Salvation." It was mandatory that the minister possess not only all of the standard theological works, but works in simple mathematics, medicine, philosophy, and the humanities, since he also often served as a tutor or schoolmaster in the colonies. It was also necessary that different views on the same subject be included, for, as Bray said, "I scarcely know one author that has so exhausted his subject as to render it unnecessary to peruse another."[1] His vital concern was to provide the clergy with the means of communicating widely useful knowledge, especially in those parts of the world where both knowledge itself, and the means of acquiring it, were hardest "to be come at."[2]

While it is true that the majority of books in the parochial libraries were theological or religious, in addition to the general literature supplied by Bray, those ministers who could afford to often added to the basic collections books that suited their own tastes. It was not Bray's aim, as he repeatedly emphasized, to supply all of the colonies and all of the ministers with complete libraries. His collections were intended to establish the libraries, and he encouraged the colonists to build upon the foundations he had provided for them. No one man could expect to provide libraries as he envisioned them without strong support and assistance from others and, as previously mentioned, Bray did not receive all of the support he had hoped for.

During the period from 1695 to 1699 covered in the first accounting to the Society for the Promotion of Christian Knowledge, Bray sent out thirty-one parochial libraries to the colonies. Nearly all of the parishes in Maryland received one, twenty-nine having gone to that colony in 1697. A proclamation by Governor Nicholson, dated March 11, 1697, indicates that the libraries had actually arrived in the colony at that time, for it provided that "all parish vestries are to return account of Books in their libraries," and "all will comply with this command or will answer to the contrary at their peril."[3] Bray continued to send libraries to the colonies until 1704. He tried repeatedly to get catalogs of the collections made and sent to him, but without success. This indifference on the part of the colonists was probably one of the strongest reasons for Bray's decision to withdraw from active participation in the affairs of the colonies and turn the work over to the Society for the Propagation of the Gospel in Foreign Parts.

As the parochial libraries of Maryland have been well covered in the literature, it is unnecessary to discuss them in detail. Two libraries will serve to illustrate the general nature of the collections.[4] Two lots of books were sent to St. James Parish, Herring Creek, in 1698 and 1703. The first lot was sent with the minister, the Reverend Charles Hall, and the second collection was sent directly to Herring Creek by Dr. Bray in June of 1703. The first group contained 125 titles in 141 volumes; the second was composed of catechetical lectures, tracts, and a number of works designated simply as "parcels of books." The second shipment amounted to at least 200 volumes. Many of the books were in Latin, with subjects covering whole fields of knowledge, including theology, philosophy, geography, history, and travels. The library was kept in good condition up to the Revolution, but the members of the vestry complained in 1740 that the rector of the parish would not give them the key so that they could inspect the library as directed by law. In 1789, when this vestry returned a report of the parish property to the convention of the diocese, the library was included in the inventory; by 1876, however, every "vestige had hopelessly disappeared."[5]

A small collection amounting to 69 volumes was sent to the Nanjemoy parish of Charles County in 1698. It contained 5 titles in history, 2 in mathematics, 1 in politics, 1 in education, 1 in language, 1 in gardening, and a total of 58 religious or theological works. The catalog is preserved in Bibliotheca Provincialis Americanae.

The comment made by the vestrymen of St. James Parish concerning their library in 1876—"that every vestige had hopelessly disappeared"— could be said as well about most of the parochial libraries after the Revolution. The ravages of war, and the neglect of the vestries, accounted for most of the losses, and often the rectors themselves were suspected of disposing of the books out of sheer economic necessity. In North Carolina, John Urmstone tried unsuccessfully to gain control of the Bath library for himself. He was prevented only by Speaker Moseley, who supposedly had some designs of his own on the library. The records of other parishes indicate that when a minister died, even though the members of the vestry were required to take custody of the library until a successor was named, the libraries were often sold along with the minister's personal effects. This was especially true, in later years, of the parochial libraries established by the Society for the Propagation of the Gospel; their letter books contain many references to such occurrences and the attempts of the ministers to recover the libraries. Many single volumes from the parochial libraries have been recently discovered; a great variety of them are preserved in the Maryland diocesan library at Baltimore. One such volume was originally a part of the parochial library at Albany, New York; its survival is amazing, since the library only contained 10 volumes in 1698, and could not have contained over 50 volumes by 1704, when Bray sent a further donation of books to the value of £14. This book is stamped on the cover "Belonging to ye library of Albany in New York," and a circular stamp inside is inscribed "Library of St. Paul's Parish, Baltimore." The diocesan library also contains books from the library at Annapolis, from the library at St. Paul's, from Herring Creek, and many of the other Maryland parish libraries.

Bray reported to the Society for the Promotion of Christian Knowledge in 1701 that the Reverend John Jackson had been sent to Newfoundland with seven libraries, one for St. John's and the others for the six bays along the coast, where Jackson visited and appointed lay readers for each settlement. In the same year, five men went to Maryland, each taking a library with him. Although each of them went to a parish which had a library, they took collections with them ranging in value from ten to thirty pounds. One of the ministers, Gabriel D'Emiliane, was a former Roman Catholic, and Bray sent him to Nanjemoy parish, where there were a large number of Catholics, in the hope that he could convert some of them to the Church of England. Bray provided him with a glebe and money to purchase two Negro servants because he had a large family. Unfortunately, the people of Nanjemoy treated him as an apostate, and he was finally sent to Christ Church Parish, Calvert County.[6]

Bray sent Daniel Brett to Pamplico, North Carolina, in the same year, but he proved to be a scoundrel and deserted his parish. He turned up a short time later in Maryland and Bray immediately cut off money for his support, as the Accounts show.[7] (A catalog of the library sent to Pamplico appears in appendix B.)

An interesting note appears in reference to the second year's allowance of books for the fort at St. John's, Newfoundland, which came to a total of £14. A stipulation noted that the books would be sent to St. John's if some means was found to protect them from the ravages of the French. If protection was not provided, the books would be sent instead to Harvard College for the use of the students there, "to let them into the Knowledge of the Episcopal Authors, to read which they begin now to have a particular inclination."[8]

As noted in the previous chapter, the parochial library movement did not gain much headway in Virginia, although Bray had sent the colony books to the value of £20 to establish the foundation for libraries in all the parishes. In 1700 he sent an additional twenty pounds to "augment the Parochial Libraries at the Colony of Virginia."[9] In the same year, he received a donation from Jeffry Jeffries amounting to £50.15, and with this money he purchased 70 Bibles, of which 50 were for the parochial libraries and 20 for the governor to dispose of as he saw fit. The cost of printing and packing came to an additional £2.3.6 over the original sum given for their purchase.[10] In the following year, the Accounts show another selection of Bibles were sent to the colony. One further donation, amounting to £11, was sent to Williamsburg in 1702. Along with the books went a large book press with a lock and key; customhouse fees and porter charges for carrying the books aboard ship cost five shillings.[11] In all, Bray spent slightly over £300 on books for the colony of Virginia, despite the fact that the library was never established on a firm basis.

One parochial library was definitely established in the colony, however, and the Accounts show that it cost ten pounds. The library was sent in 1702 to form an "Archdiaconal or 2d. rate Library for Mr. Wallace at

Kikotan in Virginia, to found for the use of Missionary Passengers, it being a Port of great Resort to and fro from England."[12] According to the colonial records of North Carolina, John Urmstone claimed he had given bond for this library, and that it should have been sent to North Carolina. Urmstone tried to take the books from Mr. Wallace, who refused to give them up without an order from the Society or Bray. Urmstone wrote to the Society and asked that the books be delivered to him, but finally had to admit defeat, as the Society never answered his letter.[13] Wallace died in 1714, and it was discovered that many of the books were lost. Urmstone feared that "like ill fate may attend the rest." Despite his efforts, the library seems to have remained at Kikotan.[14]

The parochial library at Newport, Rhode Island, has been attributed to Bray, to the Society for the Promotion of Christian Knowledge, and to the Society for the Propagation of the Gospel at different times. Actually two libraries were sent to Newport; the first by Thomas Bray in 1700, the second by the S.P.G. in 1704. On October 19, 1700, Dr. David Bethune signed for a collection of books to set up a parochial library at Newport. Bray mentioned him as being "Licens'd to be Minister of yt. place." Simultaneously he signed a receipt for a layman's library intended for the same place. At the last moment there was an apparent change of plans, since the Accounts reported that John Lockier was the man finally chosen to fill the Newport position. The libraries preceded Lockier, for he took with him collections for Boston and Philadelphia. In the following year, David Bethune was one of the six ministers sent to Maryland.

The catalog of the library, preserved in Bray's Bibliotheca Provincialis Americanae, indicates that it contained 19 folios, 12 quartos, and 38 octavos. On December 12, 1701, 12 additional volumes were added. In addition to the theology, this collection contained a Greek grammar, a geography, 2 dictionaries, and a book on gardening. In the layman's library were 42 theological works and 100 pastoral letters, sermons, and tracts. According to Bray's Accounts, the first parochial library sent cost £30.[15] The additions of 1701 were to cost £20, but not all of the volumes were sent at one time, as the following note indicates: "By twenty pounds in books partly sent and the rest prepar'd to be sent with the next safe opportunity to make up the library at Rhode Island worth £50, the first Books having come to £30."[16]

Lockier remained at Trinity Church, Newport, until the arrival of the official S.P.G. missionary, James Honeyman, in 1704. Honeyman brought a parochial library with him which had been supplied by the S.P.G. It cost £10, and was entirely theological in nature.

In 1702, Bray sent another collection, costing £19.13.6, to "Mr. Barclay a missionary in New England for a library at Brantry in that Country."[17] Nothing is known of the size or contents of this collection. The

Scottish Society for the Propagation of the Gospel sent two missionaries to New York in 1702, and with characteristic zeal, Bray immediately supplied them with libraries worth £14.12.6, to be housed at Albany.[18]

Altogether, Bray sent thirty-nine parochial libraries to America between 1696 and 1704, and most of them were still in existence in 1724 when a questionnaire was sent to all ministers in the New World by the S.P.G., asking about the condition of their libraries. This questionnaire, three copies of which were returned, was aimed to determine how well the libraries had been maintained. The replies proved that although some books were missing from the collections, many of the libraries still contained their original volumes.

The parochial libraries were probably safe as long as the minister remained in the parish. When he retired or moved, the library was often dispersed or lost before a new minister could be appointed, unless the vestrymen exercised their authority and took the library into custody.

The Layman's Library

Bray included a large collection of practical books and tracts to be given to the people along with the first libraries sent to the colonies. He soon realized that it would be "an endless undertaking to furnish everyone with books," and so devised a plan which would allow the books to be available to the people, without cost. This plan involved what he termed his "layman's" or lending libraries. As outlined in his second circular letter to the clergy of Maryland, this library would be under the care of the minister, who would lend the books to the members of his congregation.[19] Bray felt that it would be nearly impossible for a minister to visit all the people in his parish, since many were quite extensive in size; therefore, it was necessary to have in each parish a collection of plain and practical books for the laity, which could supply a cure for the defects in colonial public education. The most practical answer required the ministers to lend books to the people, which would better "answer the end than outright bestowing of them," for Bray held that "a book lent is more speedily read over and better digested" than those books actually owned by the readers, "more speedily because they know they must return the Book, and upon that receive another." Such a book would also be more carefully read and better digested because the people felt that, upon the minister's calling, "they will be asked to give some account of what they have read in it."[20] The layman's library would assist the minister in his teaching function, and help clear the people's minds of "confusion in what they understood of religion." Such a collection would compliment the minister's parochial library until such time as better libraries could be sent to the colonies. For the better preservation of these collections, Bray proposed that each be sent in a strong book press, to be kept in the vestry room.

Bray's outline showed the contents of such a library in two parts. The first part was the lending collection. The smaller books in this collection could be loaned for three months, but folios could be loaned for six. The second part contained a group of books and tracts to be given to the people, including a large number of prayer books and Bibles. The lending collection was divided into two parts: books for instruction, and books for bringing sinners back into the fold. The instructional books included Kettlewell, *The Christian Believer*; *The Whole Duty of Man*; Seaman's *Monitors*; Sherlock, *On Death*; Ellis, *Repentance*; Dorrington's *Familiar Guide to the Scriptures*; and others of this kind.

The second section contained books designed to restore to grace those who had fallen into sin. Each form of error had its theological remedy: for general apostasy, Cyprian's *Discourse on the Unity of the Church* was recommended. For apostasy to the Quakers, the sinner was required to read *The Snake in the Grass, The Snake in Answer to the Switch,* and Keith's *Christian Catechism.* Apostates to Roman Catholicism were directed to read Bennett's *Epitome of Discourse Against Papacy,* and *Accounts of the Cruelities Done to Protestants on Board the French Galleys, with an Exhortation to Perseverance.*[21]

The people could visit the minister at any time, and books could be borrowed during the week. The free books were often distributed at this time or placed in the pews on Sunday morning, to be picked up by the people when they came to church. This was also the way in which Bibles and prayer books were distributed to the congregations.[22]

One of Bray's chief objectives in providing the layman's library was to help the colonists resist the influx of doctrines not in harmony with the Church of England, and the spread of these doctrines throughout America. Chief among the doctrines repugnant to Bray was Quakerism, and he proposed that missionaries be sent to Pennsylvania to convert them. In this respect he was fortunate in having George Keith sent to be the first missionary of the S.P.G. to preach in those colonies in which the Quakers were most numerous. For Keith's use, Bray had collections of books similar to those in the layman's libraries placed in strategic locations along the coast, where Keith could refer to them or pass them out to his audience while he preached and argued.

Thousands of books were sent for the layman's libraries, as the Accounts indicate.[23] Such libraries were sent to all cities and towns to which Bray had sent provincial and parochial libraries, where they served as supplements to those libraries. Although they contained many duplicates, the libraries were quite extensive in the number of different titles. For example, in 1700 Bray sent two collections to North Carolina; one to Bath, the other to the settlement at Albemarle, each containing 870 volumes. When Mr. Baron went to Maryland in 1702, he took along twenty such libraries, which cost a total of £243.15.11. Other layman's libraries were sent to Boston, Newport, Philadelphia, New York, Charleston, Albany, and to towns in Massachusetts and Virginia. The cost of these collections ran into hundreds of pounds. Altogether, the Accounts list forty-two layman's libraries for the American colonies. In addition, Bray sent over 34,000 books and tracts, which were given away free.

That the books intended for the layman's libraries did not always find their way into the hands of those entitled to receive them is clear from a letter written by the Reverend Mr. Rainsford of North Carolina to John Chamberlayne, the secretary of the S.P.G., in 1712. He first complained that he had not received the books sent for his own use, then went on to relate that "Madam Hyde, the wife of the governor, sold me all the books committed to her care for butter and eggs, when they were to be disposed of gratis." He intimated that his fellow clergyman, Urmstone, was doing the same thing with the books in his care.[24] Despite such incidents, however, most of the books reached their intended readers, and probably had a considerable effect upon people whose reading perforce consisted only of the Bible and a few small treasured volumes brought from England. Long after Bray ceased active participation in the work of the colonies, letters continued to pour into the offices of the societies asking for books of the kind supplied in the layman's libraries, and many of the missionaries reported the good effect such books had on the populace, bringing them into the churches and away from the sins of heresy and apostasy. Such letters, continuing into the decade following the Revolution, are found by the hundreds in the manuscripts of the Society for the Propagation of the Gospel in Foreign Parts.

On the whole, because the parochial and layman's libraries were closer to the people, they touched their lives more intimately than did the provincial libraries, which often remained closed to them, depending on the whim of a minister or the actions of a colonial legislature. If the libraries had no effect, the S.P.G. would not have continued sending such reading matter to the colonies in an amount estimated to exceed 100,000 volumes. Such a quantity in itself testifies to the literary needs of the colonists, needs that Bray and the Society tried as best they could to fill. Although the letters of the S.P.G. missionaries are not excessive in their enthusiasm, the books assisted them in winning the battle against intellectual poverty, and helped instill a sense of basic Christian morality in the colonists.

Chapter 8
The Society for the Promotion of Christian Knowledge

Efforts intended to establish the Anglican church in America were made throughout the seventeenth century, but on the whole were so insufficient that at the close of the century, "in many of our Plantations, Colonies, and Factories beyond the seas . . . the provision for ministers was very mean." Many of the colonies were "wholly destitute and unprovided of a Mainteynance . . . and the Publick worship of God." And, for lack of such support and maintenance, many of the colonial subjects were well on their way to "Atheism and Infidelity."[1]

The basic fault lay in the fact that the action taken was isolated and individual, and consequently lacking in the elements of real permanence. Although much of this individual effort was undoubtedly restrained or wasted, it did, however, serve to kindle a missionary spirit, with the coincident realization that unified action on the part of the Church was necessary. From this realization emerged the religious society movement of the late seventeenth and early eighteenth centuries, culminating with the Society for the Promotion of Christian Knowledge and the Society for the Propagation of the Gospel in Foreign Parts.

Background

The earliest attempt to form such a society was presented in the "Petition of William Castle exhibited to the High Court of Parliament now assembled for the Propagating of the Gospel in America and the West Indies, and for settling our Plantations there."[2] This petition, presented in 1641, carried the names of "Seventy Able English Divines" and "some worthy Ministers of Scotland." It pointed out England's great neglect in the spreading of the gospel to America. England had been remiss in "performing this so religious, so great, so necessary a work." The author then outlined his reasons for the Church to pursue his plan: the nation would achieve advantages in commerce, and the general well-being of the colonists would be improved by this missionary effort as well. Evidence indicates that no action was ever taken on the petition.

Another contemporary missionary effort enjoyed better results. John Eliot was engaged in missionary work among the Indians of New England and New York, and through his writings, published in England, his work became well known. His efforts so impressed the Long Parliament that on July 27, 1649, an ordinance was passed establishing "A Corporation for the Promoting and Propagating the Gospel of Jesus Christ in New England." A general collection was made throughout England and Wales, and realized nearly £12,000, of which £11,000 was invested in property in England, and the missionaries among the Indians of New York and New England subsequently maintained from the income on this investment. The Society bought two libraries in 1651 for Eliot's use. They had been left behind by two Massachusetts ministers who had returned to England, Thomas Jenner, minister of Weymouth, and Thomas Weld, minister at Roxbury.[3] At the 1660 Restoration, the Corporation was declared defunct, but soon revived as "The Company for the Propagation of the Gospel in New England and parts adjacent in North America." A new charter was obtained primarily through the efforts of the Honorable Robert Boyle, who became the Company's first governor. It continued to operate in New England until 1775; after the eleven-year interval caused by the Revolution, its functions were removed to New Brunswick in 1786. This was the first missionary society established in England, and was generally known as the New England Company. As reconstituted in 1662, the society was limited to forty-five members, made up both of Churchmen and Dissenters.[4]

In England during the 1670's, the existence of "Infamous clubs of Atheists, Deists, and Socinians," laboring to propagate their "pernicious principles," caused some members of the Church of England to form themselves into societies. Young Anglican clerics and laymen began to meet weekly for religious conferences and mutual edification. Soon after this movement's inception over forty-two such religious societies were reported in London and Westminster alone. Encouraged and supported by a majority of the bishops and the Crown, the societies soon spread throughout England. Members, for the most part, were of the Church of England, and drew up their rules and orders in accordance with the Book of Common Prayer.[5]

These religious societies, in addition to the Society for the Reformation of Manners, founded in 1691, were the direct antecedents of the two religious societies founded by Thomas Bray. The Society for the Reformation of Manners was composed of non-Conformists, as well as members of the Church of England, and usually confined itself to "putting the law into opposition against Profaneness and Debauchery."[6] A common zeal for increased public morality formed the mutual working basis of both the religious societies and the Society for the Reformation of Manners, and they frequently united whenever prevailing vices called for correction or reformation of public manners. Such serious-minded people must have regarded the mass of their fellow Englishmen as having fallen into such "barbarous ignorance," such vile and "unchristian practice crying aloud for vengeance," that a new evangel was needed to reclaim them.[7]

Bray's Plans

Such a man was found in Thomas Bray, who was from the first one of the staunchest supporters of the religious societies. After his appointment as Commissary for Maryland in 1695, Bray mapped out plans for a chartered society which he called "A General Plan or Constitution of a Protestant Congregation, or Society for the Propagation of Christian Knowledge."[8] The Society was to be incorporated by royal charter, so that it could lawfully receive and invest funds. It was to be composed of two-thirds of notable London clergy, the remaining members to be "eminent for their work and affection to religion and the Church of England." The Archbishop of Canterbury and the Bishop of London were to be the leaders, represented normally by chaplains, ex officio. The members of the Corporation were to consult together about promoting religion in the plantations, to find suitable clergymen for ordination by the Bishop of London for work in the colonies, to aid in setting up libraries in the colonies, and to provide support for missionaries.

The scheme was presented to the Bishop of London in 1697, but difficulties in obtaining a charter proved too great, and the plan was laid aside. Bray had accumulated so much work by this time that he was unable to handle it alone. Consequently four of his friends formed themselves into a voluntary society at a meeting held at Lincoln's Inn on March 3, 1699, in the rooms of Serjeant Hooke. Before this first meeting, the men had already contributed £430 to Bray for the libraries.[9] In addition to Bray and Hooke, the other original members included Lord Guilford, son of Sir Francis North, Sir Humphrey Mackworth, and Maynard Colchester. These five men, in the midst of the "visible decay of Religion in the Kingdom" and with the increase of "Deism, Prophaneness and Vice," began on the "8th day of May in 1699" their humble efforts to raise the nation from its state of spiritual degradation.[10] It is noteworthy that Bray was the only clergyman among the original members. At this first meeting, the members voted to accept liability for the £631 deficit which was still owed to Bray for the libraries he had sent out to the colonies. Their records show that most of this money was repaid.

Activities

The Society for the Promotion of Christian Knowledge had a direct affect on the American colonists through its assistance to Dr. Bray in raising money for the libraries and finding ministers for the Bishop of London to send to the colonies. In a letter to Governor Nicholson in Virginia in October, 1700, John Chamberlayne, then secretary of the S.P.C.K. wrote: "The main part of their design, with relation to America, is to assist Dr. Bray in raising libraries and to distribute practical books and tracts to the laity."[11] The Society also paid for the maintenance of many of the clergymen sent to the colonies: during the three years it was directly involved in missionary enterprise, its members provided support for twenty-eight missionaries.[12]

Edmund McClure felt that "the educational work of the Society no doubt was its main business if not its *raison d'être* at the outset."[13] The Society early began publishing and translating religious works and distributing them to the needy, a task it has continued to the present. Many of the Society's publications found their way to the colonies, either in the layman's libraries or through direct donation. Guided by the plans outlined in Bray's "Design for a Lending Library in Every Deanery in England and Wales," the Society for the Promotion of Christian Knowledge gathered together collections of books which were to supply that design. Their main work in the library field was done in England and Wales, and on October 28, 1701, the members voted that "the subscriptions for the Plantations shall henceforward cease."[14] On November 4, they sold their share in Mackworth's mining venture for £200. They continued in library work in England until 1704, when the project was turned over to an ad hoc committee. The minute books of this committee, entitled "The Proceedings of the Trustees for erecting Parochial Libraries and promoting other Charitable Designs," is still preserved in the archives of the S.P.C.K.[15]

At the first meeting of the committee, Bray was appointed to provide a list of all parishes in England with an income of less than £20 per year. He was able to complete the survey with the help of the bishops, and the Society attempted to subscribe supplementary income to the poorer parishes and to provide each minister with a library.

Meanwhile, the Society continued to grow, adding such men as John Chamberlayne, its first secretary, and later secretary of the Society for the Propagation of the Gospel in Foreign Parts; Robert Nelson, nonjuring author of *Feasts and Fasts* and other religious works; John Evelyn, diarist, founder of Charity Schools, and supporter of the Society for the Reformation of Manners; and Colonel Nicholson, the professional colonial governor. Through its members, the Society was able to acquire large quantities of books, and many authors contributed their own works freely. Bray gave 500 copies of his *Lectures on the Catechism,* and Nelson gave freely of *Feasts and Fasts,* a book which found its way into most of the Bray libraries in America. Donations were used to buy books, often directly from the authors at a discount. In 1706, 500 copies of Kettlewell's *Christian Believer* were purchased for £125. It was generally possible to buy books at two-thirds off the published price.

The Society hired two rooms from Mrs. Kettlewell in her house on Southampton Street, and in one of them, called the Repository, a model library was stored. The trustees had to approve each book purchased, and to supply additional funds, they fined each late-comer to a meeting one shilling. The collection was moved in 1715 to London House, where the Bishop of London allowed the Society free space for storage.[16]

The work of establishing libraries had grown to such proportions by 1706 that a Parliamentary measure was thought necessary to protect them. A law was passed on April 2, 1709, through the influence of Lord Chancellor King, a friend of Bray. The law was entitled "An Act for the better preservation of Parochial Libraries in that part of Great Britain called England." Under this act, all parishioners liable to the charge of church rates were allowed to use the libraries. The act also contained elaborate rules for the protection of the libraries, but, as usual up to the time of the Public Library Act of 1855, no provision for financial support of the libraries, nor any provision for adding to them, was included.[17]

Newman's Work

Although the Society ceased its colonial activities in 1701, communication was maintained until after the Revolution. One of the chief reasons for this continued contact with America was the appointment of Henry Newman as secretary of the Society in 1708. Two years earlier, Newman had been appointed secretary of the library committee. Through Newman, the Society served for many years as agent for the purchase of books needed in America. Henry Newman was born in Rehoboth, Massachusetts, in 1670, the son of a Puritan minister whose father had named the town. He graduated from Harvard College in 1687, and received his Master of Arts degree in 1690. He served as librarian of the College from 1690 to 1693 and in 1703 went to London on business for the college, remaining there until his death in 1743.[18] Because of his friendship with Governor Dudley, he served occasionally as agent for the colony of New Hampshire from 1709 to 1720, and permanently from that time on. He met Thomas Bray on his arrival in London, and became vitally interested in his work. When the occasion arose, he accepted the position of secretary of the Society for the Promotion of Christian Knowledge. Newman continued his correspondence with his New England friends, but their dissenting beliefs often gained him rebukes from his fellow churchmen.

In addition to his work as agent for Harvard and the colony of New Hampshire, Newman served as a link between the New England scholars interested in science and the members of the Royal Society. He secured scientific apparatus for Yale, and wrote literally thousands of letters.[19] He acted as agent in gathering books from the S.P.C.K. and the S.P.G. for Jeremiah Dummer, which were sent to Yale in 1713 and 1714. Some of the members of the societies who presented books were Thomas Bray, Chamberlayne, White Kennett, author of the still valuable Bibliotheca Provincialis Americanae, the first English bibliography on America, Bromfield, Gunston, Sir John Phillips, William Whiston, William Bachin, Colonel Mapletoff, Governor Nicholson, and Robert Nelson.[20] This was the group of men whose books, filled with subtle propaganda, led to the defection of members of the Yale faculty in September, 1722. Newman also acted as agent in collecting the books that George Berkeley presented to Yale. The bill of lading which accompanied the books to Yale was signed "Shipped 30th of May, 1733 by order of the Rev. Dean Berkeley, at London. Henry Newman."[21] As he had done for Harvard, Newman collected the books for Yale which Thomas Clap called "the finest collection of Books that ever came together at one time into America."[22] A large number of the books in the collection were identical with those titles which Bray and the S.P.G. sent to the parochial libraries in the colonies.

A letter from Newman to Governor Belcher, undated, but probably written in 1735, listed a group of books and papers to be presented to "President Wadsworth and his associates" at Cambridge after Belcher had perused them. The collection included *Bellus Homo et Academicus*, issues of the *Weekly Miscellany, Grub Street Journal, London Journal*, and the *Daily Post Boy*, as well as sermons by the Bishop of Litchfield given before the S.P.G., Dr. Knight's sermon before the Society for the Reformation of Manners, and Mr. Smith's *Sermon before the Trustees of Georgia.*[23]

The books collected by Newman for America doubtlessly had a decided influence on the development of intellectual curiosity in the colonies, as did those sent by the Society for the Promotion of Christian Knowledge during the years that Society acted as colonial agent. A study of the mass of Newman papers in the archives of the S.P.C.K. testifies to his personal influence in all phases of colonial intellectual life.

Chapter 9
The Society for the Propagation of the Gospel in Foreign Parts

Thomas Bray's greatest achievement, considering its overall effects on the American colonies, was his Society for the Propagation of the Gospel in Foreign Parts. When the plan for a chartered society had to be laid aside in 1697, Bray continued working towards it through the Society for the Promotion of Christian Knowledge.

The Founding

The matter was finally taken under consideration by the Church, and on March 13, 1701, a committee was appointed in the Lower House of Convocation of the Province of Canterbury to inquire into ways and means of "Promoting Christian Religion in our Foreign Plantations."[1] Bray, with his usual burst of energy, ignored the committee and presented a petition directly to King William III on March 15. Although the petition was signed by Bray alone, the request doubtlessly had the full backing of Bishop Compton and Archbishop Tenison of Canterbury, since the latter donated twenty pounds to the Society for the Promotion of Christian Knowledge to defray Bray's expenses in drawing the petition, and declared that it would have the "greatest consequence imaginable" in the establishment of religion in America.[2]

The question of the new society was taken up by the S.P.C.K. on May 5, 1701, and a draft of the charter was read. The names of the officers were agreed on, and several supporting papers prepared. On June 23, Bray was able to place the charter of the new society before the members and thanks were tendered to him "for his great care and pains in procuring the grant." At the same time, "a form of subscription for raising the money due to Dr. Bray upon account of the Plantations" was adopted, since his Accounts had been audited and the Society found that "there still remained due to him £200, part of a greater sum" advanced by him towards the propagation of Christian knowledge on the continent of North America, "that these said sums had really been expended by him upon that account," and that "divers Ministers" had been sent over, as well as "many Parochial Libraries."[3]

Made up largely of members of the S.P.C.K., the new society held its first meeting on June 27, 1701, at Lambeth Palace, where officers were elected, new members welcomed, and the bylaws, standing orders, and a seal decided on. Later meetings were held in Archbishop Tenison's library in St. Martin's in the Fields.[4]

Scope of Activities

It was through the distribution of books that the S.P.G. began its work in the plantations. The first act of this kind occurred some months before the first minister was sent to America: the event was reported by the Bishop of Hereford at a meeting in February, 1702, as the sending of a "great Welch Bible and Common Prayer Book to the Welch congregation in Pennsylvania."[5] For many years, the Society was a missionary, Bible, and religious tract society in one.

The appointment of a missionary involved a mission library and books for free distribution among the members of the congregation as well. The salary allowed a minister in the beginning was fifty pounds a year guaranteed for three years, and ten pounds to buy books for each year of a three-year period. Books to be distributed free would require five pounds a year.[6]

On August 15, 1701, the S.P.G. entered upon an inquiry into the religious state of the colonies, and information was sought and obtained from trustworthy persons at home and abroad, from the Bishop of London, from English merchants trading with the colonies, from ship captains, colonial governors, and the congregations in the colonies. When this information had been gathered and studied, the Society began raising a special fund for propagating the Gospel in the colonies.

The Society appointed George Keith as its first missionary in 1702, and he sailed from England on April 24, 1702, with orders to report on the state of religion in the colonies. Among his fellow passengers were Colonel William Dudley, Governor of New England; Colonel William Morris, Governor of New Jersey; and the Reverend John Talbot, chaplain of the ship. Talbot was so impressed with Keith's undertaking that he enlisted as his companion. The party landed at Boston on June 11, and Keith and Talbot set out on their journey. They stopped to preach at every opportunity, and inquired into the spiritual condition of the people. They converted Quakers and tried in general to awaken a sense of Christianity in all of the people they met. How well Keith accomplished his objectives in the colonies is fully told in his *Journal,* published soon after his return to England.[7]

Through its study of colonial conditions at the beginning of the eighteenth century, the S.P.G. could report that in 1701 there were 43,880 members of the Anglican church in the colonies, and 50 clergymen. From 1702, when the first missionary was dispatched, until 1785, when the Society ceased operations in America, 309 clergymen were sent to the colonies, £227,454 was expended in providing libraries and paying salaries, and over 130,000 Bibles, Common Prayer Books, and other works of devotion and instruction were distributed, as well as an "innumerable quantity of small tracts." In withdrawing from the mission field in the United States in 1785, the Society arranged for the continuance of the salaries for the missionaries still officiating up to Michaelmas of that year, and undertook to provide "to the utmost of its power" for such of them as elected to "repair to any of his Majesty's Dominions in America."[8]

As might be expected, the Society for the Propagation of the Gospel in Foreign Parts concentrated its efforts in those colonies where the Church of England was not established by law. Under the Society's auspices, no parochial libraries were sent to Maryland, but several were sent to the other Middle and Southern colonies. (See appendix A, table 3, for the libraries established by the S.P.G.) Most of the efforts of the Society were concentrated in New England, New York, and the Delaware and Pennsylvania regions, but at least three libraries were established in Virginia, one at Manicantown on the James River, one at Bruton, and the third, worth fifteen pounds, was sent to a Mr. Pritchard in 1704. The catalog of the Manicantown library, the only one that survives for the colony, is printed in appendix B.

In 1701, only two Anglican clergymen served in New England: Samuel Myles at Boston, and John Lockier at Newport. At that time, the S.P.G. reported the population of the area as follows: Massachusetts, 70,000; Connecticut, 30,000; Rhode Island and Providence Plantation, 5,000; Narragansett, 3,000; New Hampshire, 3,000; and Maine, 2,000.[9]

The first congregation to receive encouragement from the Society was the parish at Newport, Rhode Island, whose church received "£15 for a Chalice, Patten, Cloath, and other necessities."[10] The Reverend James Honeyman was appointed pastor of the church in 1704, replacing John Lockier, and remained at Newport for nearly half a century. Honeyman brought a library with him to Newport, and the S.P.G. sent him additional books in 1734. There was also a parochial library established by the Society at Providence in 1721.[11]

In February, 1702, after reading letters "deliver'd in by Dr. Bray," the Society ordered that a missionary should be sent to the Narragansett country. It was not until 1706, however, that Christopher Bridge arrived there. He had served for some years as assistant rector of King's Chapel in Boston.[12]

In the beginning, the Society planned to give each of its missionaries a library worth thirty pounds, but due to the difficulties in raising the necessary funds while supporting its missionaries, the allowance was soon cut to ten pounds. The book collections were built up in London and sent along with the missionaries when they embarked for the colonies. It was not unusual, however, for missionaries already established in the colonies to request books from the Society, and in most cases, the requests were promptly filled. The letters of the missionaries show that the men often requested specific titles for their libraries, and when they were financially able, they paid for the books themselves. The fine collections that many of the ministers were able to build up over the years, based on the small foundations supplied by the S.P.G., are amazing. Some of the churches today still have the remains of the original parochial libraries, but only a few have managed to maintain and add to them substantially down to the present.

Massachusetts Libraries

The Letter Books of the S.P.G. indicate that a minister coming into a parish often had great difficulty in obtaining the library from his predecessor or his heirs. For example, the ministers of Braintree seem to have had difficulties with their libraries for a period of nearly sixty years. When the Reverend Ebenezer Miller arrived in that Massachusetts town in 1726, he wrote to the Society at once, requesting an order to obtain the parochial library from the Reverend Mr. Mossom, who was about to depart for Virginia. The Reverend John Graves wrote to the secretary of the S.P.G. in 1764 asking what was to be done with a collection of books sent to him from England for the use of Dr. Miller, the rector of Braintree, since he had recently died. In reply, the secretary ordered him to send the books on to Mr. Winslow, who had succeeded Miller.[13]

The same David Mossom who served at Braintree also served for a time as minister at Marblehead. He reported to the Society in 1724 that the books belonging to his predecessor were not there when he arrived, save for "six volumes which I keep in good order."[14] The library at Marblehead was added to from time to time; Alexander Malcom wrote in 1747 thanking the Society for a bundle of books, and the Reverend Mr. Bours did the same in 1759.[15] A short time later, Bours died, and a long exchange of correspondence took place between his successor, Joshua Weeks, and the secretary of the S.P.G. Weeks reported that Mrs. Bours had only given him half of the books in the library and had gone off to Rhode Island to marry Mr. Fayeweather, the minister there. He then wrote to Mr.

Fayeweather, who replied that he had not received the rest of the books, and thus presumed them lost. Later, Fayeweather did return one additional volume, and Weeks reported to the Society that he had recorded it with the others. He also asked the secretary to send him additional books for his library. The secretary replied that some were being sent, but in 1766, Weeks wrote again complaining that he had not received any of the promised books.[16] Finally, in 1767, the Society agreed to "supply Mr. Weeks with books to meet the deficiencies in his library."[17] Mr. Weeks must have received the books at last, for there is no further correspondence in the files concerning the library at Marblehead.

Under the direction of the Reverend East Apthorp, Cambridge had a fine library, many of the volumes purchased by Apthorp through the Society. After he left the mission the library suffered, and in two letters to the Society in 1783, Samuel Parker of Boston reported that he had managed to save several books from the library, including Herbert's *Country Parson* and Humphrey's *Historical Account of the S.P.G.*, and he now had them in his possession, along with the church plate. Parker imagined that the library had contained many more volumes, but they were lost or plundered by the American soldiers when they took possession of the house of Mr. Serjeant, Apthorp's successor.[18]

Daniel Addison, in his life of Edward Bass, quoted a letter from Bass, the minister at Newburyport, to the secretary of the S.P.G. in which he reported that he had the library from Cambridge in his possession, and wished to know what to do with it.[19] He was told to turn the books over to Mr. Parker, and eventually Parker gave the collection to Mr. Wiswall, the minister at Falmouth. Wiswall shortly afterwards left Falmouth to take charge of missions at Cornwallis, Horton, and Wilmot in Nova Scotia. "There would be no impropriety," wrote the secretary of the Society, "in transferring it to another place where the Society has a mission." He felt sure that Dr. Apthorp could have no objection to such an application of his library.[20]

Wiswall seems to have had a hand in another of the parochial libraries as well, for when Mather Byles became rector of Christ Church in Boston in 1768, one of his first duties was to write to the Reverend Mr. Wiswall at Casco Bay, Maine, "desiring him to return to this Church any books he has belonging to the Church, particularly a large Bible."[21]

When Timothy Cutler defected from the Congregational fold at Yale in 1722, he was sent to England for ordination and returned as minister of Christ Church, Boston, in 1723. His reply to the questionnaire about libraries on January 4, 1724, indicated that he had a library at that time. Cutler often wrote to the Society requesting books, and in September, 1740, when ecclesiastical Boston was shaken to its very roots by the arrival of the Reverend George Whitefield, an evangelical preacher then aged twenty-five, Cutler hurriedly wrote requesting books to counteract his teachings. One year later, he wrote: "The Society does much to oblige their missionaries by the good books they send them, especially those occasioned by the disorders and confusions Mr. Whitefield and his disciples have wrought among us."[22]

In June of 1742, a note acknowledging receipt of a parcel of books at Christ Church was recorded in the church minutes. The Reverend Mr. De Chair in England left his personal library to the church in 1746, but the books did not arrive in Boston until the following year. In 1752, it was ordered that Giles Tidmarsh make a catalog of the collection, and his listing records 53 titles in 84 volumes. Of these, 30 titles still remain in the library, including Captain Steven's *History of Spain* and Marcellini's *Roman History* in Latin.[23] Cutler was succeeded by Mather Byles, who had been librarian of Harvard College during the period from 1755 to 1757. Being interested in the library, Byles immediately had an inventory taken and discovered that, although many of the volumes had been lent, very few of them had ever been returned. At a meeting of the vestry on July 5, 1769, it was agreed that an advertisement should be inserted in the newspaper "desiring all persons that are possest of any books belonging to this Church's Library to return them." The advertisement appeared in the *Boston Evening Post* on July 31, August 7, and August 14, 1769, and was worded as follows: "Whereas a number of Books belonging to the Library of Christ Church in this Town are missing; those Persons who have them in their possession are desired to return them immediately."[24]

Mather Byles also discovered at this time that several volumes from the library had been lent to a Mr. Oliver of Salem in 1746, and he considered issuing a summons to have them returned. Byles continued as rector of Christ Church until the night of April 19, 1775, when the lanterns were hung in the church steeple as a signal to Paul Revere; the following day he left for New Hampshire. He intended to remain in the country, but in 1776, bedeviled by the Americans because of his strong Tory sympathies, he left for Halifax, Nova Scotia, where he continued to serve the church for many years.

A catalog of the library made in 1916 listed 92 volumes remaining of the original collection, among them Puffendorf's *Law of Nature and Nations*, Mede's *Works*, Baker's *Chronicles*, Schuckford's *Sacred and Profane History*, Denham's *Psalms*, and a great number of bound tracts and sermons. Though there is no record that Mr. Oliver of Salem ever returned the volumes he borrowed from the Christ Church library, a letter from his predecessor at Salem, Charles Brockwell, to the Society in 1739, reported that Salem had a library which actually belonged to the town of Scituate. How he obtained the library, he did not explain.

Despite the constant frustrations testified to in many of the letters, the fact that these collections were of vital importance to the missionaries emerges from the reports of their battles with Dissenters, Quakers, and evangelists like Whitefield, whose eloquence drew many to him out of sheer enthusiasm. Letters testifying to the good effects brought by distribution of small tracts on keeping the congregations within the churches were written by many of the missionaries. Such letters came from the Middle colonies and the South as well, where Whitefield had made strong inroads on the established Church membership. In South Carolina, it was reported that the Society had provided 2,000 volumes and about £300 worth of small tracts.[25]

North Carolina Libraries

Of all the colonies, North Carolina received perhaps the smallest supply of libraries and books. With the exception of the library established by Thomas Bray at Bath in 1700, the people of the colony had few places to turn for books, since few private libraries of any consequence existed in the whole area. One library was owned by Edward Moseley, and John Urmstone related that he had brought a library with him worth fifty pounds when he came to the colony, although it was soon lost through want of safe custody. Many of Urmstone's statements indicate that he was not entirely trustworthy, but it is probably true that he had a library of sorts. Rainsford and Gordon, colleagues of Urmstone who usually officiated around Chowan, had libraries and distributed tracts to the people with good results.[26]

When James Adams returned from North Carolina to England in 1710, he left a large collection of books in the possession of Richard Sanderson of Currituck. Rainsford attempted to get possession of the library, but Sanderson would agree to give it up only if Rainsford would settle in Currituck, as the rules stated that he could surrender it only to the minister of the parish. Rainsford wrote to the S.P.G. reporting the fact, but the books remained in Currituck.

John Urmstone also had designs on the collection, but withdrew from the battle without the books, as would anyone, he reported, who "was not musket proof."[27] From references to him throughout the period, he seems to have led a most disreputable life. He turned up in 1722 at Christ Church in Philadelphia and officiated there for one year until his conduct, which was described by a member of the vestry as "not proper to be mentioned or allowed in any sober society," caused the vestry to dismiss him from the living. Urmstone refused to leave Philadelphia, and finally the vestry had to pay him to go. From Philadelphia he moved to Maryland, and in the following year turned up drunk at a convocation of the clergy. He was deprived by the commissary.[28] In 1731, he was burned to death while "in a state of intoxication."[29]

One additional library was sent to North Carolina by the Society. The Reverend Richard Marsden, laboring in the Cape Fear region in 1735, complained to the Society that he did not have a library and that few books were to be had in the colony. He believed that it would be "a great act of charity to supply this part of the province at least with good books." He felt he could more easily combat dissent if he had books with which to refute those persons who were furnishing many families with "Bigg, Jubb, and Walstone on our Saviour's miracles and several others of the same pernicious kind."[30] The Society took its time in complying with the request, and it was not until 1755 that a library was sent to him at St. James Parish. The Society added to the collection in 1770. The *Colonial Records* testify that the Society continued to send additions to the North Carolina libraries until the Revolution, but no new libraries were established there after 1755.

With literature in such short supply in the colony, it is thus likely that these collections were the only books available to a large majority of the population for nearly 100 years. The constant flow of letters requesting books indicates that the people received them with appreciation. There is little doubt of their importance in the eyes of the clergy, who wrote of their effectiveness in combating ignorance, heresy, and vice in a colony which, according to William Byrd, was infected with these disreputable qualities in great abundance.

The Burlington Library

One of the largest and most general of the parochial libraries provided by the S.P.G. was the one started in 1702 in Burlington, New Jersey.[31] This library achieved its distinction for several reasons: first, it was established at a time when a minimum of thirty pounds was made available to the missionary. Second, it was one of the libraries enriched by a large collection of books and tracts provided to combat the Quakers, many of whom eventually became a part of the congregation. Third, the library was well supported, because the city of Burlington was one of the sites chosen as the future home for an Anglican bishop. Finally, the rector of the church was extremely interested in the collection, and added to it whenever he had the chance.

John Talbot, the first rector of St. Mary's Church in Burlington, arrived in America in 1702 with George Keith, and accompanied him on his excursion to convert the Quakers. After he returned from his trip through the South, Talbot preached in Burlington on August 22, 1703, delivering the first sermon given in the new church. He returned to England in 1705, and the congregation at Burlington petitioned the Society that he be appointed their rector. He was installed as rector of the church and returned as minister there in 1707. He wrote to the Society in June, 1709, and after discussing the state of religion in the colony, he ended with this fervent postscript: "Pray for God's sake send some books of all sorts, especially Common Prayer Books!"[32]

A catalog of the library was made in 1719 by John Talbot and Michael Piper, a schoolmaster connected with Christ Church, Philadelphia.[33] At that time, the collection amounted to some 197 titles, in addition to 55 titles which belonged to Talbot personally, and 26 titles of Quaker books which had been left for George Keith. Beyond the usual theological works, the library contained volumes in the Greek and Latin classics, dictionaries, works of philosophy, science, and history, and a number of French books. Talbot's own collection was roughly of the same composition, but with a higher percentage of theological works. (A catalog of the collection appears in appendix B.)

After nearly twenty-five years of service, Talbot was suspended by the Society in 1724 until such time as he could clear himself of charges brought by John Urmstone. On his removal from Christ Church, Urmstone swore to the Society that Talbot was a Jacobite, and secretly a nonjuring bishop. He made the same charges against Dr. Weldon, who succeeded him at Christ Church. Urmstone claimed Talbot had caused his removal from the church as part of a Jacobite plot. Strange as the story was, the Society believed enough of it to suspend both Talbot and Weldon.

The value of this, and all of the other parochial libraries sent out to America by Dr. Bray and the Society for the Propagation of the Gospel in Foreign Parts, is best summed up in the remarks made by Bishop Doane of New Jersey during the course of an episcopal address delivered in May of 1834 in Burlington:

> The Library of St. Mary's Church, Burlington, lately increased by the bequest of part of Dr. Wharton's books, is about to be brought into more general use. The remark is sometimes made that parish libraries are little used, and soon dispersed; and the fact is adduced that, of the excellent collections with which all our parishes, by the wise provision of the Venerable Society for the propagation of the Gospel in foreign parts, were furnished, are now, with scarcely an exception, squandered. Of this unfortunate result, the vicissitudes of the times ought always to be given in explanation; and it should also be remembered that the good seed, though scattered, is not lost, but producing doubtless in many quarters, its desirable fruits.[34]

Chapter 10
The Bray Associates

Once the two great religious societies had been given a firm foundation, Dr. Bray gradually withdrew from active participation in their meetings. He was content to let them go their own way, knowing that his beloved designs would continue as long as the societies lasted. Over the years he continued to receive bequests and gifts personally, and these he administered himself, with the aid of a few friends.

In 1723, the long-awaited bequest from D'Allone, amounting to something over £900, arrived at the same time that he was taken dangerously ill. He felt it necessary to form a group which could competently administer the D'Allone bequest for education of the Negroes in America, and consequently several of his friends banded together to establish the group known as Dr. Bray's Associates. These men agreed to act as trustees for the D'Allone legacy, to assist Dr. Bray in founding and supporting libraries for the clergy and lay members of the Church of England, and to help in the founding of Negro schools in the colonies.[1]

For several years, Bray had been interested in prison reform, the reclamation of fallen women, and the settlement of the poor debtors of London. Because of these interests, he met and became a strong supporter of James Oglethorpe, M.P. for Haslemere and member and chairman of the Parliamentary committee on prison reform. According to the letter of Thomas Coram, the originator of the famous Foundling Hospital in London and a member of the Associates himself, Bray first suggested the idea of a colony for debtors to Oglethorpe.[2] Whatever the source of the idea, Bray did appoint twenty-four trustees, in addition to those mentioned above, mostly at the suggestion of Oglethorpe. Bray prepared a feoffment which devolved the trust upon this greatly enlarged group of Associates, and their authority was confirmed in 1731 by a decree in Chancery.[3]

Soon after Bray's death on February 15, 1730, Oglethorpe proposed to the Associates that they apply for part of the legacy of a certain Joseph King to be used for the establishment of a "charitable Colony for the better maintenance of the poor of the city of London."[4] The members agreed, and on July 30, they presented a petition to King George II seeking a grant of land for a new colony, to be located south of Carolina. By December of 1730, the plan for the new colony lacked only Parliamentary approval for its successful inception. The petition was favorably received by the king and he signed a charter in May of 1732. The charter was delivered to the trustees on June 20, 1732.[5] All of the members named in the petition were members of the Bray Associates, but when the colony came into being in 1733, two distinct groups developed within the Associates. Both continued to share the same offices and the same secretary for several years. Since many of the trustees were interested in neither the Christian education of Negroes nor the spread of parochial libraries in England, save for Coram and Percival, Oglethorpe added the money he received from the king's bequest to the money Bray had received from D'Allone in order to finance the new colony. Of the two groups, the Trustees for Georgia devoted themselves completely to the plans for the colony, while the Bray Associates began their work in the conversion and education of Negroes and the development of parochial libraries. In May, 1733, Percival, who continued to be a member of both groups, ordered that an inventory be made of Bray's books, and Mr. Smith, Mr. Hales, and Doctor Bedford were appointed to "inspect and make a report of the books" and give their private opinion as to "how they should be disposed." Lord Percival suggested that where they discovered "too many of one sort" they should be exchanged for others so that they might form "more complete libraries."[6] From the beginnings of their work in the parochial library field, the Associates were on good terms with the members of the Society for the Promotion of Christian Knowledge, and were able to exchange their duplicates with them.

The Associates began their work in distributing libraries in 1734, when Governor Belcher of New England approached them for libraries to assist the missionaries working with the Indians on the borders of New England. (See appendix A, table 4, for the libraries established by the Bray Associates.) On October 9, the Associates agreed to send ten pounds worth of books to "the two Scots Missionaries sent to Convert the Indians" as requested by Governor Belcher. The missionaries, actually three in number, were Stephen Parker, Ebenezer Hinsdell, and Joseph Secomb, paid by the Scottish Society for the Propagation of the Gospel.[7] On June 25, 1735, a letter from Dr. Coleman was read to the assembled members, acquainting them with the "proceedings and character" of the three missionaries to

71

the Indians, and reported the safe arrival of "the books sent to them." At the same meeting, the second collection of books was ordered sent to form a library for the "Palatine Minister to Virginia."[8]

One of the most important acts of the Associates, exclusive of their library work in England and Wales, was the supplying of books and libraries for the new colony of Georgia. Members of all three societies presented gifts of money, materials, and literally tens of thousands of books and tracts to the colony. A complete list of all benefactions, with the names of the donors, is included in a folio volume entitled "The General Accompt of all Monies and Effects Received and Expended by the Trustees for Establishing the Colony of Georgia in America."[9]

These "Accompts" show that over 10,000 books and tracts were donated to the colony by the Bray Associates, the Society for the Promotion of Christian Knowledge, and the Society for the Propagation of the Gospel in Foreign Parts, as well as by individuals throughout England. The donations included Bibles, homilies, prayer books, hundreds of horn books, primers, "ABC's," and a group of 1,000 spelling books. The gifts included "a parcel of books in divers Faculties for the Library of Georgia," by the Earl of Egmont, and a "Parochial Library for Savannah" from the Associates. On May 5, 1736, Egmont related in his diary that "We did no business only received from Mr. Bedford a catalogue of the Parochial Library given Mr. Arnold for his church in Newhaven in New England," and they also received that minister's bond "to leave the said library to his successors in that church."[10]

Like the religious societies, the Associates did not rely only on their own members for contributions, but used all means available to seek help from persons willing to support their work. Egmont noted one such attempt in his diary entry for February 9, 1737, when he reported that an advertisement would be published in the newspapers to let the world know "we have erected twenty-three parochial libraries since the year 1730, and to invite willing people to contribute to so good a design, our fund being exhausted."[11]

After 1736, the Associates became involved in founding and adding to parochial libraries in England and Wales, and it was seventeen years before they established another library in the New World. In a manuscript of the Associates it is recorded that on August 15, 1753, they sent a library of 154 volumes to the Reverend Ottolengh in Savannah.[12] These books were to provide a library for a Negro school to be erected in that city, and the gift included psalm books, primers, and horn books. Other titles included *The Whole Duty of Man*, Nelson's *Feasts and Fasts*, Common Prayer Books, and various pious tracts. The whole collection, as was usual with libraries established by the Associates, was of a strict religious and educational nature.

Not all of the libraries sent to the colonies by the Associates were destined for the Negro schools, for several parochial libraries were also sent.[13] In all, the Associates sent forty-one libraries to the new world, of which ten were parochial, thirty were for the Negro schools, and one was a lending library. In addition, they sent special gifts of books to the Indian missionaries in New England, to King's College, to the College at Philadelphia, to Trinity Church, and to the College of William and Mary. These gifts amounted to over 20,000 volumes, including the original grants to Georgia in 1735 and 1736.[14]

The establishment of Negro schools and parochial libraries in America was given great impetus by the election of Benjamin Franklin to membership in the Associates on January 2, 1760.[15] From the beginning, they relied heavily on him for recommendations and assistance. Franklin recommended that Negro schools be established in New York, Newport, Rhode Island, and Williamsburg. He also recommended that Samuel Johnson, President of King's College, Mr. Dawson, President of William and Mary, and the Reverend Mr. Pallen, minister of Newport, be asked to take over the care and management of the Negro schools in their cities. Franklin was asked to write to those gentlemen telling them of the wishes of the Associates, and he did so immediately. Letters printed in the *Abstracts* indicate that the men were all willing to do what the Associates asked of them. These Negro schools met with rather lukewarm success in the colonies, mainly because the slave owners did not wish to have the children educated and did little to encourage their participation in the schools. A letter from Daniel Earl of Edenton, North Carolina, was typical of the dozens of letters from the teachers in the plantations showing the difficulties under which they labored. He reported that the owners were willing to have their Negroes educated, but could not spare them from their work. They also argued that the teaching of Negroes would preclude the teaching of white children, as the parents would not allow them to be educated together.[16]

In many of the parishes, especially in North and South Carolina, the towns were few and far apart, and it was nearly impossible for the teacher to collect enough pupils to open a school. Those schools which were opened in the larger cities, especially in the North, had the greatest chance of success, though here too their success was severely limited.

On May 1, 1760, Dr. Johnson attended a meeting with Franklin at Mr. Birdie's house. The records do not show that he ever attended another meeting, but he did remember the Associates, and later left to them the profits from the sale of the first edition of his collection, *Prayers and Meditations*, which amounted to £50. This collection was published posthumously by Samuel Johnson's friend, the Reverend George Strahan, vicar of Islington, in 1785.[17]

During the year 1761, Franklin served as chairman of the group, as he related in a letter to his daughter.[18] Back in New York in the following year, Franklin reported to the Associates that he had been to Williamsburg and could give a good report on the school there. He added that he intended to visit the schools in New York and Newport, and on his return to his home in Philadelphia would minutely inquire into the state of the school there.[19]

The only lending library dispatched by the Associates was the one sent to the Reverend Mr. Marge of Orange County, Virginia, on February 4, 1762, when they sent four book collections to be placed at his four places of worship for use as lending libraries for the respective congregations. These libraries contained a total of 330 volumes, of which 235 were religious tracts and works of piety, and were unbound. Mr. Marge wrote to the Associates requesting additional books, but they had to refuse his request because of a lack of funds.[20]

Parochial libraries, as a rule, were sent to those ministers who were not connected with the Society for the Propagation of the Gospel in Foreign Parts, since that body provided its missionaries with libraries. In most cases, the ministers wrote to the Associates requesting help in establishing libraries for their own use and that of their parishioners. The *Accounts* of the Associates record several groups of books sent to the Reverend Jonathan Boucher, the fiery Loyalist of the Revolution, and the *Abstracts* also contain several letters requesting books for his library. On April 1, 1762, the Associates agreed to "allot a parcel of books towards a parochial library in Hanover Parish for the use of him & his successors."[21]

One of the most interesting of the parochial libraries, primarily because of its connection with Benjamin Franklin, was the library sent to Woodbridge, New Jersey, in 1760. On November 6, the Associates received a letter from the minister at Woodbridge asking help in establishing a library. Dr. Franklin reported that he believed a parochial library would be of great service to the people there, and so it was agreed that "one copy of each of the English books in the Associates' store which Dr. Franklin approved should be given towards a library to be fixed at Woodbridge in New Jersey."[22] On January 1, 1761, Mr. Waring reported that he had prepared a packet of books and tracts to add to the library at the request of the Society for the Promotion of Christian Knowledge. The books seem to have arrived safely, for on May 10, 1761, a letter written by James Parker of Woodbridge to John Waring was read at the meeting of the Associates, in which he thanked them for the books and the gift of "a guinea to build a bookpress" to hold the collection.[23] Among other authors, this collection contained works by Bray, Allen, Kettlewell, Nelson, and Hales, and amounted to 263 volumes. (A catalog of the collection appears in appendix B.)

The Associates continued to send books to the established libraries and supplied new libraries in America until just before the Revolution. The last recorded library was sent to Northampton, Virginia, on March 4, 1771, and contained 377 volumes.[24] With the coming of Independence, the Associates shifted their efforts from the colonies to the libraries in England and Wales. They added to the libraries established by Thomas Bray and founded a number of their own. Through their efforts, over 160 libraries were founded in England and Wales.[25]

Chapter 11
Appraisal

When Thomas Bray was appointed the Bishop of London's Commissary to Maryland in 1695, the only library of any size in America was that belonging to Harvard College. A number of individuals had libraries, among them the libraries of the Mathers and William Byrd, but such libraries, as a rule, were not available to the public. Bray quickly realized that the men who came to him in answer to his call for service in the colonies were too poor to supply themselves with the books he deemed necessary for them to properly fulfill their function as Christian educators. He developed plans which would provide each of the ministers with a library, and with the aid and approval of the higher clergy, he began soliciting funds to finance them.

Originally, he had planned to provide such libraries for all of the parishes in Maryland, but as he learned of the extensive cultural poverty of the people in the colonies, he enlarged his plans to provide for one large library in the chief city of each province, the provincial or general library, and a smaller collection, the parochial library, for each of the colonial parishes. A third type of library, the layman's library, would contain books which could be loaned by the minister, and a large collection of pious books and tracts which were to be given free to the people.

From 1695, when Bray first accepted the position as commissary, until 1704, when he presented his final report to the Society for the Propagation of the Gospel in Foreign Parts, he was successful in establishing provincial libraries at Boston, New York, Philadelphia, Annapolis, Charleston, and Bath, North Carolina. He provided thirty-nine parochial libraries, of which twenty-nine were located in Maryland, although each of the other colonies had at least one such library. Finally, he provided over thirty-five layman's libraries and sent over 35,000 religious books and tracts to the colonies for free distribution.

That Dr. Bray's work was continued in America to the eve of the Revolution tells a great deal about the colonial needs for reading matter still too difficult and expensive to acquire in America. Literally thousands of letters from the colonists and their ministers, now preserved in the archives of the Society for the Propagation of the Gospel in Foreign Parts, testify to the fact that the American colonists were desperately in need of books and libraries during the eighteenth century. Bray and the societies he founded did a remarkable job in providing the colonists with the books and libraries they desired.

In supplying libraries, missionaries, and schoolmasters for the colonies in a steady stream for nearly 100 years, Bray and the religious societies sought to equalize cultural opportunities on both sides of the Atlantic. In their work with the Indians and Negroes, they tried to bring Christianity and some form of rudimentary education to those neglected peoples.

As Thomas Bray once stated with justifiable pride, he managed to lay the foundations of seventy libraries on the North American continent almost single-handedly. The libraries stretched from Newfoundland in the North to the Carolinas in the South. In addition, he provided libraries in the West Indies, on the coast of Africa, established sixty-one libraries in England and Wales, ten on the Isle of Man, and several in the highlands of Scotland. During the same years he was providing books, libraries, and missionaries for the colonies, he was instrumental in securing passage of a bill for the establishment of the Church of England in Maryland, and was active in the foundation of the Society for the Promotion of Christian Knowledge and the Society for the Propagation of the Gospel in Foreign Parts. The Bill for Establishment remained in force through the entire colonial period, and the three societies founded by Bray remain in existence today, still active in publishing, educational work, and missionary enterprise, a tribute to his zeal and thoroughness.

Bray and the societies poured literally thousands of books and tracts into the culturally barren colonies at little or no expense to the colonists themselves, and he fought for years to secure the collections, both financially and legislatively. He was gratified to see legislative protection given to the libraries in three of the colonies during his lifetime, but failed in his attempts to procure public support for their growth and development.

Bray's library plans should not be criticized on the grounds that he failed to add to the libraries or provide for their support; rather, such criticism should fall on the recipients of the libraries, who failed to add to the collections and to give them the support and protection that Bray requested. Although there was a great need for books, it is unfortunate that the kind of scheme Bray envisioned was so far ahead of its time: even so, the books that he provided could not have been better chosen to fill the needs of the clergy and the people of early eighteenth century America.

Indifference on the part of those in power often caused the benefits of these fine libraries to be lost to the people, but even had laws been made, it is doubtful that the libraries would have survived. The English library act of 1709 is a case in point. The establishment of the true public library had to wait upon the shift of support from private benevolence to public funds in the latter half of the nineteenth century. Though the colonists often requested books, Bray's library movement was an outside one, and did not spring from the people themselves. The libraries came at a time when the colonists were slowly ceasing to think of themselves as transplanted Englishmen, but rather as Americans. For one thing, the religious diversity of the colonists was working against an established religion. It is also true that the library movement was tied too closely to the Anglican church. Had the Church of England pressed its advantage from the beginning of colonization and established strong control over its colonial clergy, such an argument would have no validity; but instead the Church let the opportunity slip. When the time came to consider the establishment of a bishopric in America, the move was not only opposed by the Dissenters and Quakers, but by many of the Anglican congregations themselves, since they had assumed control of their local churches through the vestries.

Because the clergymen of the Church of England were required to take an oath of allegiance to the king upon ordination, most of them felt they could not break that oath when the Revolution came, and remained loyal to the Crown despite the hardships such action caused them and their churches. Most of the seventy libraries perished with the war, but many of them had suffered loss and neglect long before that time, because no one in authority was appointed to watch over them. There was little desire to revive the libraries after the war, for book production in America had come of age, and the tastes of the people had changed, becoming more secular.

The strong feelings of nationalism which the Revolution produced led to an interest in the development of a truly American culture, with less of an intellectual dependence on Europe, especially England. Those libraries which did survive were absorbed by other libraries more secular in nature, and were retained as curiosities or examples of English culture in colonial America.

Thomas Bray's library concepts were surprisingly modern, quite in advance of his time. Had he been born 100 years later, he would have been in the thick of the movement for the development of public libraries. In his own time, and through his own labors, a stream of the finest reading matter then available filtered into the American cultural scene.

The Society for the Promotion of Christian Knowledge, founded by Bray in 1699 and known for its cultural, ethical, and religious activities, served for many years as a link between scholars of America and their counterparts in England and on the Continent. The Society served as an agent in collecting books for men in the colonies and kept them in touch with the latest scientific and artistic developments.

The Society for the Propagation of the Gospel in Foreign Parts, established in 1701, provided libraries, schools, and missionaries to America, and with its support of the infant American colleges, it aided the spread of religion and education in the colonies for nearly 100 years. Hundreds of ministers and schoolmasters and literally thousands of pounds were sent by this Society to aid the colonial churches, schools, and libraries.

Dr. Bray's Associates, through their work in establishing schools and libraries, and their work in the conversion and education of Indians and Negroes, contributed their share to the development of an American culture which extended its benefits to oppressed and underprivileged peoples. Their interest in the resettlement of the poor debtors of London led to the establishment of the colony of Georgia in 1733.

Because of his own activities on behalf of the colonies, and because of the activities of the Society for the Promotion of Christian Knowledge, the Society for the Propagation of the Gospel in Foreign Parts, and the Bray Associates, Thomas Bray deserves credit for serving as one of the greatest single cultural influences at work in the American colonies during the eighteenth century. For his work, the United States of America owes him an eternal debt of gratitude. Few men did as much for their fellowman as unselfishly as did Thomas Bray, and few men have received less in the way of earthly recompense for their labors.

Appendixes

Appendix A: Tables

TABLE 1

Classification of the Bray Provincial Libraries:
Divine and Human Knowledge

Class		*New York*	*Boston*	*Philadelphia*	*Charleston*	*Bath*
I.	Holy Scriptures and commentaries	23	36	29	27	11
II.	Fathers	7	28	10	18	13
III.	Apologetical discourses	19	5	11	8	14
IV.	Bodies of divinity	14	13	17	23	13
V.	Covenant of Grace and Creed	18	27	24	36	3
VI.	Moral laws	28	18	20	29	3
VII.	Repentance and Divine Assistance	3	8	5	5	6
VIII.	Prayer and sacrament	10	0	22	10	9
IX.	Sermons	34	27	36	25	10
X.	Ministerial directives	5	8	9	7	12
XI.	Controversial	19	20	27	18	29
XII.	Things					
1.	Humanity	6	5	9	11	11
2.	Policy and law	0	0	1	0	3
3.	History and its appendages	23	17	19	42	5

Class	New York	Boston	Philadelphia	Charleston	Bath
4. Physiology Anatomy Surgery Medicine	2	0	30	15	1
5. Mathematics and trade	0	1	5	6	3
XIII. Words					
1. Grammars and lexicons	6	2	8	6	3
2. Rhetoric	1	0	1	0	4
3. Logic	1	0	0	0	1
4. Poetry	3	0	0	2	1
XIV. Miscellanies	6	0	2	1	12
Total volumes	211	221	327	225	166
Total nonreligious	48	25	75	83	48

SOURCE: Compiled from Bibliotheca Provincialis Americanae. Annapolis is not listed because the contents of the library are unknown.

TABLE 2

Parochial Libraries Established by Thomas Bray

Place	Date	Volumes	Additions
Maryland			
St. Mary's	1696	314	1702
Herring Creek	"	150	1703
South River	"	109	
North Sassafrass	"	42	
King and Queen's Parish	"	196	
Christ Church, Calvert Co.	"	42	
All Saints'	"	49	
St. Paul's, Calvert Co.	"	106	
Great Choptank, Dorchester Co.	"	76	
St. Paul's, Baltimore Co.	"	42	
Stepney, Somerset Co.	"	60	
Porto Batto, Charles Co.	"	30	
St. Peter's, Talbot Co.	"	10	
St. Michael's, Talbot Co.	"	15	
All Faiths', Calvert Co.	"	11	
Nanjemoy, Charles Co.	"	10	1701, 1702
Piscataway, Charles Co.	"	10	
Broad Neck, Ann Arundel Co.	"	10	
St. John's, Baltimore Co.	"	10	
St. George's, Baltimore Co.	"	10	
Kent Island	"	10	
Dorchester, Dorchester Co.	"	10	
Snow Hill, Somerset Co.	"	10	
South Sassafrass	"	10	
St. Paul's, Kent Co.	"	30	
William and Mary, Charles Co.	"	26	
Somerset, Somerset Co.	"	20	
St. Paul's, Talbot Co.	"	25	
Coventry, Somerset Co.	"	25	
Pickamaxon	1701	Cost £10	
All Hallows	1701	Cost £10	
Durham Parish (Nangemny)	1704	Cost £10	£70 pledged
New Jersey			
Amboy	1698	30	
New York			
Albany	1698	10	1704 (Cost £14)
Rhode Island			
Newport	1700	79	1701, 1704
Massachusetts			
Braintree (now Quincy)	1704	Cost £19.13.6	
Virginia			
Kikotan (now Hampton)	1704	Cost £10	
North Carolina			
Albemarle	1704	Cost £20	

SOURCE: Bray's Accounts.

TABLE 3

Parochial Libraries Established by the S.P.G.

Maine
  Falmouth (now
    Portland),
    1770–75
  Gardner, 1770–75

Massachusetts
  Boston (Christ
    Church), 1723
  Bristol (now in
    Rhode Island)
  Marblehead
  Braintree (now
    Quincy)
  Cambridge, 1759
  Newburyport
  Salem
  Taunton
  Newbury (before
    1716)
  Scituate

New Hampshire
  Portsmouth, 1736

New York
  Jamaica, 1702
  Hemstead
  Stetin (Staten Island)
  New Rochelle
  Rye
  Westchester
  Richmond
  Albany

Pennsylvania
  Chester
  Philadelphia (St.
    Peter's), 1761
  New Castle
  Oxford

Radnor, 1714
Lancaster
York
Perkiomen
Delaware
  Lewes
  Dover

Connecticut
  Stratford, 1723
  New London, 1732
  New Haven, 1736
  Litchfield,1761
  Wallingford
  Ripton (now
    Huntington)
  Norwich
  Groton
  Middletown
  New Cambridge
    (now Bristol)
  Fairfield (now
    Southport)
  Hebron
  Newtown
  Reading
  Woodbury
  Poquetanock
  West Haven
  Plymouth
  Topsham

New Jersey
  Burlington, 1702
  Amboy, 1702
  Elizabethtown, 1702
  Salem, 1725
  New Brunswick,
    1754–55
  Shrewsbury, 1702

North Carolina
  Edenton, 1723
  Bath, 1706, 1734
  Chowan, 1712
  Cape Fear (now
    Wilmington)
  Currituck, 1708
  Urmstone's library,
    which circulated
    with him

South Carolina
  St. Andrews,
    Berkeley Co.
  Charleston
  Christ Church,
    Berkeley Co.
  St. James, near Goose
    Creek, 1702
  St. James, Santee,
    1706
  St. John, Berkeley
    Co., 1707
  St. Katheryn
  Portroyall
  St. Bartholomews
  St. Thomas
  St. Helena, Beaufort
  St. George, Winyah,
    1721
  Prince Williams, 1758
  St. Michaels, 1755
  All Saints',
    Waccamaw
  St. David's, Cheraw,
    1768

SOURCE: This compilation is taken from the following sources: Perry, *History of the American Episcopal Church*; Pascoe, *200 Years*; Herbert Osgood, *American Colonies in the Seventeenth Century*; the "Queries to the American Clergy" in the Fulham Palace Manuscripts; and the S.P.G. Letter Books and Minutes, transcribed by Francis Lister Hawkes, now in the New-York Historical Society Library.

TABLE 4

Libraries Established by the Bray Associates

Location	Date	Type	Volumes
Savannah, Ga.	1735	Parochial	70
Germanna, Va.	1735	Parochial	Unknown
Newhaven, Conn.	1736	Parochial	Unknown
Savannah, Ga.	1753	Negro School	154
St. Paul's, S.C.	1753	Negro School	617
Charleston, S.C.	1753	Negro School	31
Charleston, S.C.	1761	Negro School	123
Orange Co., Va.	1756	Parochial	63
Orange Co., Va.	1757	Parochial	116
Orange Co., Va.	1762	Negro School	330
Orange Co., Va.	1762	Lending	330
Philadelphia, Pa.	1753	Negro School	271
Philadelphia, Pa.	1759	Negro School	192
Philadelphia, Pa.	1764	Negro School	170
Williamsburg, Va.	1760	Negro School	182
Williamsburg, Va.	1761	Negro School	164
Williamsburg, Va.	1763	Negro School	163
New York City	1760	Negro School	182
New York City	1761	Negro School	164
New York City	1766	Negro School	228
Newport, R.I.	1760	Negro School	182
Newport, R.I.	1768	Negro School	285
Woodbridge, N.J.	1760	Parochial	263
Edenton, N.C.	1761	Negro School	154
Bath, N.C.	1761	Negro School	123
Wilmington, N.C.	1765	Parochial	92
Frederick Co., Md.	1761	Negro School	154
King George's Co., Va.	1762	Parochial	58
Leeds, Va.	1764	Parochial	236
Yorktown, Va.	1762	Negro School	78
Norfolk, Va.	1762	Negro School	78
Chester, Md.	1762	Negro School	78
Fredericksburg, Va.	1764	Negro School	110
Fredericksburg, Va.	1766	Negro School	162
Fredericksburg, Pa.	1766	Negro School	202
Fredericksburg, Md.	1766	Negro School	333
Charles City, Va.	1769	Negro School	56
Cape Fear, N.C.	1769	Negro School	215
Taunton, Mass.	1771	Parochial	Unknown
Northhampton, Va.	1771	Negro School	377

Appendix B: Catalogs

Library of King's Chapel, Boston

A Register of Books
Sent with his Excellency the Earl of Bellomont towards laying the
Foundation of a Provincial Library at Boston in New England

I. On the Scriptures

Biblia Polyglotta   6 vols.   fol.
Castelli Lexicon   2 vols.   fol.
Robertson's Liber Psalmorum Heb.   12mo.
Bythner's Lyra Prophetica   4to.
Buxtorfii Thesaurus   8vo.
Calvini Opera et Commentaria   4 vols.   fol.
Poli Synopsis Criticorum   5 vols.   4to.
Dr. Lightfoot's Works   2 vols.   fol.
Dr. Hammond on the Psalms   fol.
Dr. Hammond on the New Testament   fol.
Mr. Baxter on the New Testament   8vo.
Chemnitii et Gerhardi Harmoniae Evangelicae   fol.
Estius in Epistolas   fol.
Mr. Joseph Mead's works   fol.
Mr. Edwards on the difficult texts together with his other works   5 vols.
Craddock's History of the Old and New Testament   2 vols.   fol.
Newman's Concordance   fol.
Wilson's Christian Dictionary   fol.
Buchanii Missionarium Theologicum   4to.

II. Fathers

Clementis Epistolae ed. Colomesii   8vo.
Polycarpi et Ignatii Epistolae   ed. Usserii Oxon.   4to.
Justini Martyris Opera, Coloniae 1686   fol.
Tertulliani Opera, Rigaltii, Paris, 1644   fol.
Cypriani Opera
Minucii Felicis
Arnobii
Julii Firmici Materni
Commodiani Opera Omnia ex. Pamelii ed. Paris 1666   fol.
Ambrosii Opera   2 vols.   Paris 1661   fol.
Athanasii Opera   Gr. et Lat.   2 vols.   fol.
Augustini Opera   7 vols.   fol.
Fulgentii Opera   8vo.
Gregorii Opera   8vo.
Bernardi Opera   fol.
Dalleus de usu Patrum   4to.
Scriveneri Apologia pro Ecclesiae Patribus   4to.

This catalog is taken from Bray's Bibliotheca Provincialis Americanae, p.3–17
(UCLA photocopy of ms. in S.P.G. Archives, London).

III. Discourses Apologetical

Grotius de Veritate Christianae Religionis   12mo.
Dr. Henry More Opera Theologica   3 vol.   fol.
Stillingfleet's Origines Sacrae   4to.
Edwards on the Authority, Style, and Perfection of
  the Holy Scriptures   3 vols.   8vo.

IV. Bodies of Divinity

Estius in Sententias, Paris, 1638
Chemnitii Loci Communes   fol.
Calvini Institutiones   *Inter Opera*
Polani Syntagma   fol.
Turretini Compendium   4to.
Phillippi a Limborch Theologia Christiana   fol.
Le Blanc's Theses Theologicae   fol.
Vosii Theses Theologicae   4to.
Dr. Hammond's Practical Discourses   fol.
Dr. Scott's Christian Life and Discourses   5 vols.   8vo.

V. On the General Doctrine of the Covenant of Grace

First Volume of the Catechetical Lectures, 1967   fol.
Short Discourse on the Doctrine of our Baptismal Covenant

VI. On the Creed in General

Dr. Jackson's Works   3 vols.   fol.
Dr. Perkins on the Creed with his other works   3 vols.   fol.
Dr. Heylyn's Theologia Veterum   fol.
Bishop Pearson on the Creed   fol.
Dr. Barrow on the Creed   8vo.
Dr. Barrow's Opuscula, etc.   fol.

VII. On the Particular Articles

Dr. Bates on the Divine Existence   8vo.
Dr. Pelling on the Divine Existence   8vo.
Mr. Edwards on Divine Existence and Providence   8vo.
Dr. Sherlock on Providence   4to.
Charnock on Providence   *Inter Opera*
Charnock on the Divine Attributes   fol.
Dr. Bull's Judicium Ecclesiae Catholicae de Necessitate Credendi
  quod Dominus Noster Jesus Christus Versus sit Deus
Dr. Barrow on the Trinity, bound up with Assheton's Collection
  upon that subject   8vo.
Bishop Stillingfleet on the Trinity   8vo.
Bishop Stillingfleet on the Satisfaction of Christ   8vo.
Dr. Sherlock's Knowledge of Jesus Christ   2 parts.   8vo.
Downame on Justification   fol.
Dr. Bates's Harmony of the Divine Attributes in the Great Business
  of Man's Redemption   8vo.
Dr. Bull's Examen Censurae   4to.
Dr. Sherlock on Death   8vo.

Dr. Sherlock on Judgement   8vo.
Drelincourt's Considerations on Death   8vo.
Allen on Justification with his Answer to Ferguson   fol.

VIII. On Moral Laws and Christian Duties

Zouche's Elementa Jurisprudentiae   12mo.
Sanderson de obligatione Conscientiae   8vo.
Bishop Taylor's Ductor Dubitantium   8vo.
Sharrock de Officiis   8vo.
Mr. Perkins's Cases of Conscience   8vo.   *Inter Opera*
Bishop Barlow's Cases of Conscience   8vo.
Dr. Cave's Primitive Christianity   8vo.
Summa Viritutum et Vitierum   8vo.
Bishop Hopkins on the Ten Commandments   4to.
Bishop Taylor's Holy Living and Dying   8vo.
Christian Monitor with Wake upon Death   8vo.
Kettlewell's Measures of Christian Obedience   8vo.
Dr. Pelling's Discourses on Holiness   8vo.
Downame's Christian Warfare   fol.
Dr. Hornbeck's Happy Ascetick   8vo.
Dr. Hornbeck's Great Law of Consideration   8vo.
Bishop Fowler's Design of Christianity   8vo.
Bishop Fowler's Christian Liberty   8vo.

IX. Of Prayer and the Sacraments

Bishop Hopkins on the Lord's Prayer   4to.
Dr. Bright upon Prayer   8vo.
Dr. Comber's Discourses on the Whole Common Prayer   8vo.
Kettlewell's Sacrament of the Lord's Supper   8vo.
Dr. Horneck's Crucified Jesus   8vo.
Dr. Horneck's On Repentance   8vo.
Dr. Goodman's Prodigal Pardoned   8vo.
Allen on Divine Assistance   *Inter Opera*
Theses Theologicae de Baptismo, etc.   8vo.
Dorrington's Familiar Guide   8vo.

X. Sermons

Bishop Andrews's Sermons   fol.
Bishop Reynold's Works, large paper   fol.
Bishop Sanderson's Sermons   fol.
Archbishop Tillotson's Sermons   10 vols.   fol.
Archbishop Leighton's Sermons   2 vols.   4to.   1 vol.   8vo.
Archbishop Leighton's Praelectiones   8vo.
Dr. Barrow's Sermons   3 vols.   fol.
Dr. Conant's Sermons   2 vols.   8vo.
Bishop Stillingfleet's Sermons   2 vols.   8vo.
Bishop Ryder's Sermons   8vo.
Dorrington's Discourses   2 vols.   8vo.
Falkner's Remains   8vo.
Dr. Hammond's Sermons   *Inter Opera*
Bishop Brownriggs Sermons   fol.

XI. Historical

Petavii Rationarium Temporum
Craddock's Church History of the Old and New Testaments   2 vols.   fol.
Dupin's Ecclesiastical History of the First Nine Centuries   3 vols.
Bishop Taylor's Life of Christ   fol.
Dr. Cave's Lives of the Apostles   fol.
Dr. Cave's Lives of the Fathers   2 vols.   fol.
Burnet's History of the Reformation   2 vols.   fol.
Quick's Synodicon, or History of the Reformed Church of France   2 vols.
Blount's Censura Authorum   fol.
Sir Richard Baker's Chronicle of the Kings of England   fol.
Varenius's Geography with Sanson's Maps   fol.

XII. Controversial

Chemnitii Examen Concilii Tridentini Francofort, 1573   fol.
Chamieri Panstratiae   4 vols.   fol.
Field, On the Church   fol.
Dr. Hammond's Polemical Discourses   fol.
Dr. Comber's Roman Forgeries   4to.
Liturgia Tigurina   8vo.
Hooker's Ecclesiastical Polity   fol.
Bishop Stillingfleet's Unreasonableness of Separation   4to.
A Stop to ye Cause of Separation   8vo.
Dr. Sherlock's Defense of the Unreasonableness   12mo.
Dr. Sherlock's Vindication of the Defense   12mo.
Bishop King's Inventions of Man in the Worship of God   12mo.
Account of Ancient Church Governments   4to.
Mr. William Allen's Works   4 vols.   8vo.
Leslie's Snake in the Grass   8vo.

XIII. Philological and Miscellaneous

Plutarchi Opera; Gr. et Lat. Francofort, 1599   2 vols.   fol.
Ciceronis Opera London, 1681   2 vols.   fol.
Epictetus; Gr. et Lat. Cum Cebetis Tabula Oxon.   1670   8vo.
Littleton's Dictionary   4to.
Scapula's Lexicon   fol.
Leybourn's Cursus Mathematicus   fol.
Introductio ad Chronologiam   8vo.
Lamb's Great Suit against Independency   8vo.

XIV. Ministerial Directories

Mr. Dodwell's Letters for the Susception of Holy Orders   8vo.
Mr. Baxter's Gildas Salvianus   8vo.
Penton's Apparatus Theologia   8vo.
Bishop Burnet's Pastoral Care   8vo.
Bibliotheca Parochialis   4to.
The Clergy's Honour in the Life of St. Basil and St. Chrysostom   4to.
Daily Office for the Sick   8vo.

A Catalogue of Books sent August 14, 1701 to Boston
in New England to Augment ye Library there for the
use of ye Church of England Ministers

Mori Opera Philosophia   2 vols.   fol.
Dr. H. More Exposition of Daniel   4to.
Dr. H. More Apocalypsis Apocalypseos
Dr. H. More Answer to Sevl. Remarks to his Expos. to Daniel and Apocal.
Dr. H. More Illustration of Daniel and Revelation
Dr. H. More Ds. on Several Texts
Defense of the Snake
Book of Psalms with argumt. of each Psalm
Moxon's Mathematical Dictionary
Five Discourses by the Author of the Snake

This catalog is taken from Bray's Bibliotheca Provincialis Americanae, p.18
(UCLA photocopy of ms. in S.P.G. Archives, London).

Library at Bath, North Carolina

A Catalogue of Books sent Dec. 2, 1700 with Mr. Brett Towards
Founding a Parochial Library at St. Thomas' Parish, Pamplico,
North Carolina

Folio

Poole's Synopsis Criticorum   5 vols.
Mede's Works
Dr. Hammond's Works   4 vols.
Maldonatus in 4 Evangelia
Scapula Lexicon Graeco Latinum   1652
Philipii A. Limborch Theologia Christiana
Works of the Author of the Whole Duty of Man
Ductor Dubitantium
Causin's Holy Court
Downham on Justification
Petri Martyris Loci Comimes
Sir Richard Baker's Chronicles of the Kings of England
Horvel's Lexicon Tetraglocton (English, French, Italian, Spanish.)
Wilkin's Real Character
Pearson's Exposition on the Creed
Merchant's Map of Commerce
Chillingworth's Religion of Protestans a Safeway to Salvation
Quillim's Display of Heraldry
Laud Against Fisher
Towerson on Creed, Lord's Prayer, Sacraments   4 vols.
Davis de Jure Uniformitatis Ecclesiasticae
Case Against the Dissenters by the London Divines
Churchill's Divi Britannici
Monasticum Anglicanus Epitomiz'd
Cambridge Concordance
Barrow's Sermons
A Church Bible

Quarto

Bibliotheca Parochialis
Bibliotheca Catechetica
Athias's Hebrew Bible
Littleton's Dictionary
Turretini Compendium
Pagit's Christianography
Thorndike's Weights and Measures
A Way to Get Wealth incl. 6 Principal Vocations
Hornbeck de Conversione Iudorum et Gentilium
Le Grand's Historia Natura Varius Experimentis
Pet. Molinaei Anatome Arminianismi

This catalog is taken from Bray's Bibliotheca Provincialis Americanae, which also
contains the catalogs of eighteen other libraries sent to America.

Goodman's Penitent Pardon'd
Discourses on Notes on the Church
A Religious Conference on Baptism
Claud's Historical Defence of the Reformation
Sparrow's Collection of Canons
Parker's Demonstration of Divine Authority of Christian Religion and
    Laws of Nature
Kettlewell's Measures of Christian Obedience
Stillingfleet's Irenicum
Keith's Four Narratives and Other Tracts
    1. Arguments Against Baptism and ye Supper Answer'd
    2. Satan Disrobed
    3. History of Sin and Heresy
    4. Parallel Betwixt Quakers & Heretics
    5. Quakers Set in True Light

Octavo

English Bible with Apocrypha & Service
Corpus Juris Civilis Gottofridi
H. Simon History & Original Progress of Ecclesiastical Revenues
Dr. Bull Judicium Ecclesiae Catholicae
Justinus cum Notis Variorum
Whiston's New Theory of the Earth
Virgil cum Notis Variorum
Falkner's Libertas Ecclesiastica
Horace cum Notis Variorum
Epictuetu's Morals with Simplicius's Command
Burnet's Abridgement of the History of the Reformation
Wharton's Reflections on Ancient and Modern Learning
Jurieu's History of the Council of Trent
Gentleman's Recreation in Four Parts, viz Hunting, Hawking, Fowling,
    Fishing
Seller's History of Palmyra
South's Sermons   3 vols.
Osborn's Advice to his Son
Five Discourses of the Author of the Snake in the Grass
The Snake in the Grass
Defence of the Snake
Huetii Demonstratio Evangelica   2 vols.
Grotius's Truth of the Christian Religion
Rawlet's Divine Poems
Sanderson On Episcopacy
Hickman's Animadversions on Dr. Heilius' Quinquarticular History
Oxford Grammar
Mr. Clark's Three Practical Essays
Life of Dr. Thomas Smith
Varenii Descriptio Regni Japonica et Siam
Galaei Opuscula Mythologica Ethica et Physica Gre. Lat.
Goodman's Winter Evening Conference   2 vols.
Varenii Geographia Universalis
Le Comle's Journey Through the Empire of China

Kettlewell's Discourses
Richardson's New Testament Vindicated against Toland's Amyntor
Whaley's Sermons of Adultery and Christian Warfare
Hill's Municipium Ecclesiasticum
Drellingcourt's Christian Defense
Hudibras 1st. & 2nd. parts
Bishop Wilkin's Sermons
Peirce's Paceficatorium
Whartoni Historia de Episcopis et Decanis Londoniensibus
Sherlock's Practical Discourses
Payne's Sermons
Wake's Principles of the Christian Religion
Wingate's Abridgement of Statutes in Force until 1641
Stillingfleet's Vindication of the Trinity
On the Suffering and Satisfaction of Christ   2 vols.
Bates's Harmony of Divine Attributes
Bishop Usher's Power of the Prince
Second Part of the Whole Duty of Man
Whaley's Sermons
Boyle's Enquiry into Vulgarly Held Notions of Nature
Verstigan's Antiquities
England's Worthies
Mathew Poole on ye Nullity of the Romish Faith
Christian's Pattern
Burnet's Vindication of the Church and State of Scotland
Sherlock's Practical Christianity
Buxtorfii Lexicon Hebraicum et Chaldaicum Balilese
Juvenal's Satyrae cum Notis Variorum
Wingate's Arithmetick
Maurice's Defence of Diocessan Episcopacy
Guilielmi Grotii Enchiridion de Juris Naturalis Principius
New and Easy Method to Understand Roman History
Turner's Middle Way betwixt Necessity and Freedom
Ken's Reasonableness of Christian Religion
Observations on a Journey to Naples
Historical Collections Concerning Changes of Religion in the Reigns
    of Henry & Edward VI, Mary & Elizabeth
Scott's Works   5 vols.
Bishop Patrick On Repentance
Passor's Lexicon Craeco Latinum
Holder's Discourses
Ars Cogitandi sive Logica
Mr. Allen's Catholicism
Busbali Graecae Gramatico Rudimenta
Mandey's Marrow of Mesuring in Glazing, Painting, Plastering, Masonry,
    Joyners, Carpenters, Bricklayers
Dugard's Vindication of the Marriage of Cozin Germane
Boull's Pandaemonium or Blow to Modern Sadducism
Boyle's Medicinal Experiments
Christian Education of Children

Burnet's Letters with His Reflections on Varillay's History of the Revolutions
Art of Heraldry
The Penitent or Entertainments for Lent
Easy Methods with Deists and Jews
Bodini Respub. Aristotl.
Buxtorfii Epitome Gramaticae Hebrae
Art of Speaking
Manger's French Grammar
French New Testament
Chassonaei Enchiridion Juris Civilis
Short Discourses on the Baptismal Covenant
Dr. Willis's Advice to the Roman Catholics of England
Angliae Notitia sive praesens status Anglicae Succinte Enucleatus
Ellissi Oratii de Principius Juris Naturalis Enchiridion
King's Inventions of Men

Library of Manicantown, Virginia

A Catalogue of the Parochial Library at Manicantown, on the
James River, in Her Majesty's Colony of Virginia, 1710

Bishop Reynold's Works, London, 1679.
Divi Cypriani Opera, Paris, 1619.
The Book of Homilies, Oxford, 1683.
The Book of Common Prayer, London, 1709.
Archbishop Tillotson's Works, London, 1707.
Bishop Sanderson's Sermons, London, 1689.
Allen on Faith, London, 1703.
Allen On ye Two Covenants, London, 1703.
Kettlewell's Practical Believer, London, 1703.
Dr. Bray's Lectures on ye Catechism, London, 1703.
Bishop Taylor's Life of Christ, London, 1657.
Dr. Parke's Commentary on Joel, Oxford, 1691.
Cambridge Concordance, Cambridge, 1692.
The Ecclesiastical History of Eusebius, London, 1650.
Bishop Usher's Body of Divinity, London, 1658.
A Review of the Council of Trent, London, 1638.
Bishop Hopkin's On the Lords Prayer, London, 1692.
A Common Place Book on the Holy Bible, London, 1697.
Lacantii Opera a. Tho. Spark, Oxford, 1694.
Nelson's Feasts and Fasts, London, 1707.
Dr. Lucas's Sermons, 2 vols., London, 1698.
Gastrell's Christian Institutes, London, 1707.
Gastrell's Certainty of the Christian Revelations, London, 1699.
Dr. Scott's Sermons, 2 vols., London, 1698.
Dr. Blackhall's Sermons on Several Occasions, London, 1708.
Concerning ye Holy Scripture by ye Author of Whole Duty of Man, Oxford,
    1678.
Bishop Burnet's Pastoral Care, London, 1692.
Camfield, Of Angels, London, 1678.
Spincke's Trust in God and Worthington's Resignation, London, 1696.
Bonnel's Life, London, 1701.
The Art of Contentment by the Author of the Whole Duty of Man, Oxford,
    1675.
The Government of the Tongue by ditto, Oxford, 1675.
Bishop Wilkin's Gift of Preaching, London, 1699.
The Whole Duty of Man, London, 1686.
Thomas a Kempis in English, London, 1701.
Harrison's Exposition of ye Church Catechism, London, 1708.
Herbert's Country Parson, London, 1652.

This catalog, the only record of a library sent to Virginia by the S.P.G., appears
in "List of Books Sent to the Colonies," S.P.G. Manuscript B, 1:93–94, S.P.G.
Archives, London.

Library of Burlington, New Jersey

A Catalogue of Books Belonging to Burlington Library Revised
By Mr. John Talbot Incumbent & Mich: Piper ye
25th Day of March 1719

Folio

1. D. Johanne Avenario Egrano Lexicon Hebraicum.
2. Scapulae Lexicon.
3. Eusibii Ecclesiast Histor.
4. ~Gregorii Sayr Casus Conscient.
5. Newman's Concordance.
6. Seti Cypriani Opera.
7. Petri Ravenelli Bibliotheca.
8. Father Paul's History of Council of Trent.
9. Pierceson on the Creed.
10. Dr. Bray's Lectures.
11. Cowleii Opera.
12. Hooker's Eccles. Polity.

Quarto

1. Riveli Controversiae.
2. Patrick upon Genesis.
3. Pindari Traged   2 vols.
4. Stillingfleet's Unreasonables of Seperation.
5. Bythneri Lyra Prophetica.
6. Skinner's Opticks.
7. Patrick on ye Chronicles, Ezra, etc.
8. Boyle's Lectures.
9. Dallei Latinorum Cultus   2 vols.
10. Cainet Dominical.
11. Littleton's Dictionary.
12. Origine Sacra by Stillingfleet.
13. Cluverii Geographica.
14. Two Manuscripts.
15. Discipuli Sermones Quadragesimales.
16. Lubini Comment on Juvenal.
17. Higgin's Sermons.
18. Senecae Traged.
19. Common Place Book Manuscr.
20. Calvin's Institutions.
21. Quintilian.
22. Juvenal cum notis Variorum.
23. One Manuscript.
24. Stierii Logica.
25. Manuscript Greek.
26. Young's Sermons   2 vols.
27. Virgil in Usum Dephini.
28. Gassendi Astronomica.
29. Sherrock's Jus Naturae.
30. Horatius in Usum Delphini.
31. Plinii Epistolae.
32. Senecae Controversiar.
33. Bp: Hall's Episcopacy by Divine Right.
34. Seaman's Monitor.
35. F: Lewis de Granada Memorial of a Christian Life.
36. Bp: Symon's Paraphrase on ye Psalms.
37. Bernardi Vareni Geographia.
38. Walker's Particles.
39. Bragg's Discourses.
40. Renati des Cartes Philos.
41. Rheault Physicks.
42. Westminster Grammar.
43. Moor's Discourses on Several Texts.
44. Senecae Philosophia.
45. Plauti Comaedae   2 vols.
46. Stapleton's Promptuarium.
47. Sherlock on Providence.
48. Matthew Kellison Survey of Religion.
49. Art of Speaking.
50. Quintiliani Institutiones.
51. Mahomet's Alcoran.
52. Defence of Catholick Faith.
53. Pererii Comment on Daniel.
54. George Where's Method of History.

This catalog appears in S.P.G. Manuscript B, vol. 1, S.P.G. Archives, London.

55. Musae Oxoniensis.
56. Natalis Comes.
57. Robinson's Key to ye Hebrew Bible.
58. Bercheli Catechismus.
59. B. Brancis de Sales Love of God.
60. Buxtorf's Lexicon.
61. Ciceronis Apothegmath.
62. Euclid's Elements.
63. Fullies Epistles.
64. Cook's Guide to Blessedness.
65. Leusden's Compendium.
66. Hogg's Poems.
67. Janua Linguarum.
68. Norris his Discourses.
69. Epitome Grammaticae Hebrae Buxtorfi.
70. Ross's Florilegium.
71. Patrick's Paraphrase of Job.
72. Sophiclia Tragediae.
73. Homer's Illiads.
74. Moor's Dialogues.
75. Guilliandi Collatin in Epistolae Pauli.
76. Dr. Hammond's Fundamentals.
77. Suiceri Physica.
78. Homer's Illiads.
79. Irenicum Magnum.
80. Fabriani Stradae Prolusiones Academicae.
81. Buxtorfi Epitome Grammat Hebraecae.
82. Scripta Publiae Proposita.
83. Didaci Stellae de modo Concionandi.
84. Epitome Erasmi Adagiorum.
85. Epictoli Enchiridion.
86. Manuscript.
87. Pagor's Lexicon   2 vols.
88. Magiri Philosophia.
89. Steuneti Hebraea Grammatica.
90. Statii Poemata.
91. Gradus ad Parnassum.
92. Ovidii Metamorphosis.
93. Baronii Metaphysica.
94. Chamberlain's Present State of England.
95. Catechism Council of Trent.
96. Anthologia.
97. Manuscript.

98. L'Art de Connoitre.
99. Isocratis Orationes.
100. Robinson's Phrases.
101. History of Polindo, &.
102. Poetae Minores.
103. Posselii Colloquia.
104. Eckii Homiliae.
105. Heckermanni Logica.
106. Eustachii Philosophia.
107. Vosseii Epigrammata.
108. Facquet's Arithmetick.
109. Sebastiani Dictionarium Hebraicum.
110. Laurentius Valla.
111. Aesopi Fabulae, Gr.
112. Decretalia Romana.
113. Pia Hilaria.
114. G.P. Safeguard from Shipwreck.
115. Sanderson's Prelections.
116. Hebrew Psalter.
117. Fereneo Minnit.
118. Erasmi Copia Verbor.
119. Brig's Opticks.
120. Mr. Jus. Fiat Lux.
121. Isocratis Orationes.
122. Horace. Bond.
123. Owen's Concordance.
124. Pythagoras his Golden Verses.
125. History of Elias Neau.
126. Ovid de Arte Amandi.
127. Lucian's Dialogues.
128. Needham's Collections.
129. Aesop's Fables.
130. Catechism Gr. & Lat.
131. French New Testament.
132. Virgil.
133. Greek Grammar.
134. Barelaii Argenis.
135. Farmer's Catechism.
136. Walker's Logick.
137. Cornelius Nepos.
138. Tulii de Officiis.
139. Vosaii Rhetorica.
140. Parker's Apology for Des Cartes.
141. Textor's Epistoles.
142. Oliani Historia.
143. Wendelini Theologia.
144. Horace, Juvenal, & Perseus.
145. Greek Grammar.

146. Caroni Apostolatus.
147. Lucius Florus.
148. Plutarchus de Educandia Liberis.
149. The Rehearsal transpos'd.
150. Burgerdicii Logica.
151. Barker Orationes.
152. Aphthonii Progymnasmata.
153. Higlen's History.
154. Radan Orator Extemporarius.
155. Vigerii Idiomata.
156. Greek Manuscript.
157. Cornelius Nepos.
158. Demosthenis Orationes.
159. Gerardi Meditationes.
160. Vindiciae pro Nicholao Smitheo.
161. The Right Way to Health & Long Life.
162. Pontani Aureum Diurnale.
163. Thomas a Kempis.
164. Formulae Oratoriae.
165. Moriae Encomium   2 vols.
166. Busquebius de Moribus Turcarum.
167. Auli Gellii Noctes Atticae.
168. Summae Conciliorum.
169. Aprippae Cornelli de Vanitate.
170. Treleatis Loci Communes.
171. Hodder's Arithmetick.

172. Farnabie's Rhetorick.
173. Martial's Epigramas.
174. Conciones et Oration ex Historia, &.
175. Lett concerning Toleration.
176. Nonnus his Poems.
177. Erasmi Select. Colloquia.
178. Barclai Euphormion.
179. Historia Anabaptista.
180. Mori Enchiridion Ethicum.
181. Introduction a la vie Devote.
182. Valerius Maximus.
183. Ambrosius de Officis.
184. Corvini Jurispruden.
185. Sleidan.
186. Treatys of the blest Sacrament.
187. Oweni Epigrammata.
188. Gobianus de Morum Simplicitate.
189. Martialis Epigram.
190. Caesar's Commentari.
191. Novum Testamentum.
192. Paraphrasis Psalmor.
193. Spirituale Direct.
194. Les Sages Entretien.
195. Small Hebrew Book.
196. Drexelius Nuntius Mortis.
197. Small French Book.

Library at Woodbridge, New Jersey

Catalog of Books Sent to Found a Parochial Library at Woodbridge, New Jersey, November 1760 by the Associates of the Late Dr. Thomas Bray

Allen on the Covenant
Bray's Catechetical Lectures
Nelson's Feasts and Fasts
Hales's Exposition on the Catechism   2 vols.
Kettlewell On the Creed
Scot's Christian Life   5 vols.
Holy Bible
6 Indian Instructed
6 Scriptural Catechism
10 Easy Method of Instructing Young
4 Bacon's Four Sermons to the Masters
4 Bacon's Two Sermons to the Slaves
11 vols. of Religious Tracts
Coney's Companion to the Sick Bed
Faith and Practice of a Church of England Man
Kettlewell's Obedience
Goodman's Pentinent Pardoned
Sherlock's Sermons
Hickes's Apologetical Vindication
4 Burkitt's Help and Guide
Dr. Berriman's Sermons   2 vols.
Dr. Clarke's Practical Essays on Baptism
3 Stebbing's on the Catechism
6 Christian Guide or Whole Duty of Man
Ken's Manual
10 Church Catechisms
4 Preliminary Essays Towards Rending Exposition on the Catechism Useful
2 Worthington's System of Christian Doctrine
Distilled Spirituous Liquors the Bane of the English Nation
Church Catechism with Scripture Proofs
12 Admonitions to the Drinkers of Gin
Easy and Delightful Method of Family Religion
Common Prayer, octavo
Osterwald's Arguments   3 vols.
Wake's Exposition of the Catechism
3 Great Importance of a Religious Life
Bonnel's Life
Whole Duty of Man, large
Gibson On the Sacrament
Stebbing On Prayer
4 Discourses on Death and Judgement
25 Osterwald's Necessity for Reading the Scriptures
12 Gibson on Devotion

This catalog is taken from Bray Associates, "Catalogues of Books for Home and Foreign Libraries, 1753–1807." S.P.G. Archives mss., London.

25 Exhortation to Housekeepers
25 Pastoral Letters From a Minister
25 Husbandman's Manual
3 Gibson's Two Letters to Masters and Mistresses of Negroes
12 Gibson's Letters Against Euthenasia
6 Gibson's Letters Against Swearing
6 Gibson's Letters Against Intemperance
12 Gibson's Letters on Serious Advice After Sickness

Notes

Chapter 1

1. *Colonial Society of Massachusetts Publications* (Boston: The Society, 1907), 12:116–31.

2. Franklin B. Dexter, *A Selection from the Miscellaneous Historical Papers of Fifty Years* (New Haven, Conn.: Yale Univ. Pr., 1918), p.223–34.

3. Samuel Morison, *Harvard in the Seventeenth Century* (Cambridge, Mass.: Harvard Univ. Pr., 1936), 1:295.

4. Cotton Mather, *Magnalia Christi Americana . . .* (Hartford, Conn.: Andrews, 1855), p.243.

5. *Massachusetts Historical Society Collections*, series 2 (Boston: The Society, 1843), 10:172.

6. Thomas G. Wright, *Literary Culture in Early New England* (New York: New York Univ. Pr., 1956), p.126.

7. Jesper Svedberg, *America Illuminata* (Spara, Sweden: n.p., 1732), 163p.

8. John Campanius Holm, *A Short Description of the Province of New Sweden* (Philadelphia: M'Carty & Davies, 1834); Israel Acrelius, *A History of New Sweden; or, the Settlement on the Delaware*, trans. by William Reynolds (Philadelphia: Historical Society, 1874), 478p.

9. Acrelius, *A History*, p.194.

10. *Ibid.,* p.366.

11. James Truslow Adams, *A History of American Life* (New York: Macmillan, 1928), 3:115–19.

12. Louis B. Wright, "Pious Reading in Colonial Virginia," *Journal of Southern History*, 6:382–92 (Aug. 1940); Wright, "The Purposeful Reading of Our Colonial Ancestors," *ELH, A Journal of English Literary History*, 4:85–111 (June 1937); George K. Smart, "Private Libraries in Colonial Virginia," *American Literature*, 10:24–62 (Mar. 1938).

13. Frank Klingsberg, "Contributions of the S.P.G. to the American Way of Life," *Church Historical Society Publication* (Philadelphia: The Society, 1943), 14:37.

14. Thomas Bray, *An Essay Towards Promoting All Necessary and Useful Knowledge* (London: printed by E. Holt for Robert Clavel, 1697), p.12.

15. *Ibid.,* p.12, 18.

Chapter 2

1. The earliest basic life of Bray is the anonymous *Public Spirit: Illustrated in the Life and Designs of the Reverend Thomas Bray* (London: J. Brotherton, 1746). The sketch in the *Dictionary of National Biography* and the recent life by Henry Thompson, *Thomas Bray* (London: S.P.C.K., 1954), are based largely on this source. An excellent short study is John Wolfe Lydekker, "Thomas Bray, Founder of Missionary Enterprise," *Historical Magazine of the Protestant Episcopal Church*, 12:86–224 (1943).

2. William Blades, *Books in Chains and Other Bibliographical Papers* (New York: Armstrong, 1892), p.41.

3. Joseph Parker, *Alumni Oxoniensis: The Members of the University of Oxford, 1500–1714* (London: Parker, 1891–92), 1:173.

4. Thompson, *Bray*, p.4.

5. *DNB*, 11:1315, under Lloyd. Lloyd was one of the seven bishops whose trial in 1688 was a prelude to the Revolution. He was very much interested in the clergy under his charge, and encouraged catechetical instruction.

6. Thomas Bray, *The Whole Course of Catechetical Instruction* . . . , 5 parts (London: W. Hawes, 1702).

7. William S. Perry, *Historical Collections Relating to the American Colonial Church*, vol. 4, *Maryland* (Hartford: privately printed, 1870–78).

8. Maryland, box 141, Fulham Palace mss. (Library of Congress photocopy).

9. The contents of this and the preceding volume are discussed in chapter 3.

10. Thomas Bray, Accounts, pt. 2 (1701–2), p.13, C. Hoare & Co. mss., London (author's photocopy).

11. *Public Spirit*, p.23.

12. Sion College mss., p.215–24 (Library of Congress photocopy).

13. Thomas Bray, *A Memorial Representing the Present State of Religion on the Continent of North America* (London: William Downing, 1700), p.4.

14. Baltimore: Evan Jones, 1700; this is said to be the first surviving Maryland imprint.

15. *The Acts of Dr. Bray's Visitation held at Annapolis, Maryland May 23, 24, 25, anno 1700* (London: William Downing, 1700), p.7.

16. Letter to Major Dent, Chelsea, March 10, 1702/3, Sion College mss., p.244–45.

17. *Calendar of State Papers*, Colonial Series. *America and the West Indies* (London: His Majesty's Stationery Office, 1910), p.299.

18. Thomas Bray, *Several Circular Letters to the Clergy of Maryland* . . . (London: William Downing, 1701), p.3. His Accounts (pt. 2, p.3) show that he paid a Mr. Hall of Herring Creek £10 in 1701 for inspecting libraries in Maryland.

19. S.P.G. *Journal*, 1:1–3. S.P.G. Archives mss., London.

20. Bray, Accounts, pt. 2, p.12.

21. Perry, *Historical Collections*, 4:57–63.

22. *Ibid.*, p.64.

23. Thomas Bray, *For God or for Satan* (London: William Downing, 1709), 16p.

24. Thomas Bray, *The Good Fight of Faith* (London: H. Hills, 1709), 27p.

25. Act of Anne c.14, Cap. XIV, printed in Church of England, Central Council for the Care of Churches, *Parochial Libraries of the Church of England* (London: Faith Pr., 1959), p.48–50.

26. Perry, *Historical Collections*, 4:71.

27. For a good discussion of this collection, see Samuel C. McCulloch, "Thomas Bray's *Missionalia,*" *Historical Magazine of the Protestant Episcopal Church* 16:27–34 (Sept. 1946).

28. *Notes and Queries,* 6, no. 163:558 (Dec. 11, 1852).

29. City of Birmingham, *99th Annual Report of the Public Libraries Committee* (Birmingham: The Committee, 1961), p.8.

Chapter 3

1. Ernest Hawkins, *Historical Notices of the Missions of the Church of England in the North American Colonies* (London: Fellowes, 1845), p.16.

2. First thought to have been printed around 1700, but *see* Lawrence Wroth, "Dr. Bray's *Proposals,*" *Massachusetts Historical Society Publications* 54:518–34 (1932). Wroth shows eleven editions, 1695–1700.

3. William S. Perry, *History of the American Episcopal Church* (Boston: Osgood, 1885), 1:138.

4. Bibliographical description of the various editions of these *Proposals* is very involved, as shown by the Wroth study. For this paper, the edition printed in the first edition of *Bibliotheca Parochialis* in 1697, and occupying p.121–30 of that volume, is used, and all references are to that edition.

5. Thomas Bray, *Bibliotheca Parochialis,* pt. 1 (London: printed by E. Holt for Robert Clavel, 1697), 130p.

6. *Proposals,* p.124.

7. Thomas Bray, *An Essay Towards Promoting all Necessary and Useful Knowledge Both Divine and Human, in all Parts of His Majesty's Dominions, Both at Home and Abroad* (London: Robert Clavel, 1697), 22p.

8. Thomas Bray, *Apostolick Charity, Its Nature and Excellence Considered* (London: W. Hawes, 1699), p.iv.

9. *Ibid.,* p.ii–iv.

10. Thomas Bray, *A Memorial Representing the Present State of Religion on the Continent of North America* (London: William Downing, 1700), p.2.

11. *Ibid.,* p.2.

12. Photocopy of a transcription from the Lenox Collection in the New York Public Library, in the writer's possession.

Chapter 4

1. Until 1952, the only copy of the Accounts thought to have survived was one in the archives of the S.P.G. In 1952, while working on his life of Bray, Henry Thompson discovered a second copy in the possession of the Bray Associates, and in 1961, this writer was able to secure a microfilm copy of a third version from C. Hoare & Co., London bankers. This bank was founded by goldsmith Sir Richard Hoare in 1672, and his son, Henry, who succeeded him in the business, was a member of the S.P.C.K. When Bray published his *Proposals,* he directed that all contributors send their money to Mr. Henry Hoare of Fleet Street.

2. *Proceedings and Debates of the British Parliament Respecting North America,* ed. by Lee F. Stock (Washington: Carnegie Institute, 1927), 2:219.

3. Edmund McClure, *A Chapter in English Church History, Being the Minutes of the S.P.C.K.* (London: S.P.C.K., 1888), p.131.

4. Great Britain. Privy Council, Colonial Series. *Acts of the Privy Council, A.D. 1680–1720* (Hereford: His Majesty's Stationery Office, 1910), 2:320.

5. Great Britain. Public Record Office, *Calendar of Treasury Books, Oct. 1697–Aug. 1698* (London: His Majesty's Stationery Office, 1933), p.161.

6. *Ibid.*, 18:237.

7. Thompson, *Bray*, p.35.

8. *Calendar of State Papers*, Col. Ser. *Am. & W.I.* 1:154 (May 1693–Oct. 1697).

9. *Ibid.*, p.529.

10. *Ibid.*, 2:47.

11. McClure, *A Chapter in English Church History*, p.73.

12. *Ibid.*, p.167, 234.

13. *Ibid.*, p.77.

14. *Ibid.*, p.21.

15. *Ibid.*, p.31.

16. *Ibid.*, p.143, 151, 154, 195.

17. *Ibid.*, p.495.

18. Bray, Accounts, pt. 2, p.6.

19. *Ibid.*, p.16.

Chapter 5

1. Bray, Accounts, pt. 1, p.4.

2. Chelsea, August 27, 1703, Sion College mss., p.236–41.

3. Perry, *History of the American Episcopal Church*, 1:416.

4. James Doyle, *The English Colonies in America* (New York: Holt, 1907), p.73.

5. Thomas Newcome, *The Life of John Sharp, Archbishop of York* (London: n.p., 1825), 1:352.

6. Arthur L. Cross, *The Anglican Episcopate and the American Colonies* (New York: Longmans Green, 1902), p.101. *See also* Carl Bridenbaugh, *Mitre and Sceptre: Transatlantic Faiths, Ideas, Personalities and Politics, 1689–1775* (New York: Oxford, 1962), for a good discussion of the colonial bishopric.

7. *The Lives of those Eminent Antiquaries John Leland, Thomas Hearne, and Anthony a Wood* (Oxford: University Pr., 1772), 1:8–9.

8. John Aubrey, *Letters Written by Eminent Persons in the Seventeenth and Eighteenth Centuries* (London: Longman, Hurst, 1813), 1:117.

9. *Calendar of State Papers*, Col. Ser. *Am. & W.I.* 129 (May 15, 1696–Oct. 31, 1697).

10. *Ibid.*, p.155.

11. Sion College mss., p.108–9a.

12. Bray, Accounts, pt. 1, p.39.

13. South Carolina (Colony). Assembly, *Journals of the Commons House of Assembly* (Columbia: Historical Commission, 1914), 7:13.

14. *Ibid.*, 8:6.

15. *Ibid.*, p.14.

16. *Ibid.*, p.18.

17. South Carolina, *Statutes at Large*, 8:16.

18. This law appears along with several others in effect in the colonies at that time in Nicholas Trott, *The Laws of the British Plantations in America, Relative to Church and Clergy, Religion and Learning* (London: B. Cowse, 1721), p.90–94. As noted above, Nicholas Trott, the Attorney General of South Carolina, was one of the original commissioners of the South Carolina Library board.

19. *See* chapter 6, "The Provincial Library."

20. South Carolina, *Statutes at Large,* 2:374–76.

21. Sections 19–32 of chapter 52 of the *Revision of the Laws of North Carolina* (New Bern: The Assembly, 1752). Rainsford reported that in 1712 the library had been "all dispersed and lost by those wretches that do not consider the benefit of so valuable a gift." North Carolina, *Colonial Records* (Raleigh: Hale, 1886–90), 1:860.

22. Edward Ingle, "Parish Institutions of Maryland," *Johns Hopkins Studies* (Baltimore: Johns Hopkins, 1883), 6:44.

23. Theodore Gambrall, *Church Life in Colonial Maryland* (Baltimore: Lycett, 1885), p.91–92, 104–11.

Chapter 6

1. Established by Governor Nicholson in 1696, built in 1697–98.

2. *Calendar of State Papers,* Col. Ser. *Am. & W.I.* (May 15, 1696–Oct. 31, 1697), p.123.

3. Morris Radoff, *Buildings of the State of Maryland at Annapolis* (Annapolis: Hall of Records Commission, 1954), 9:10.

4. *Calendar of State Papers,* Col. Ser. *Am. & W.I.* (1700), p.220.

5. Radoff, *Buildings,* p.26.

6. *Ibid.,* p.28.

7. *Calendar of State Papers,* Col. Ser. *Am. & W.I.* (May 15, 1696–Oct. 31, 1697), p.126.

8. *Ibid.,* p.128.

9. *Ibid.,* p.47.

10. "The Reverend Thomas Bray and His American Libraries," *American Historical Review* 2:73 (1896–97).

11. *Ibid.,* p.74.

12. Bray, Accounts, p.9. "Fifty pounds in promise was still owed."

13. South Carolina (Colony), *Journal,* 7:28.

14. *Ibid.,* p.36.

15. *Ibid.,* 6:27. The layman's library contained 1,500 volumes. Accounts, pt. 1, p.16.

16. *Ibid.,* 19:20.

17. *Ibid.,* 11:106.

18. *Ibid.,* 12:90.

19. *Ibid.,* p.9. Trott wrote a letter of thanks from the House.

20. "Documents concerning the Reverend Samuel Thomas, 1702–1707," *South Carolina Historical and Genealogical Magazine* (Charleston: Historical Society, 1904), 5:24. Nicholson was a strong supporter of Bray's schemes for years, and gave money for books, churches, and support of ministers in Rhode Island, North Carolina, and South Carolina. He gave books to the College of William and Mary, and left his library to the S.P.G. to be given to that college at his death.

21. *Carolina Chronicle: The Papers of Commissary Gideon Johnston,* ed. by Frank J. Klingberg (Berkeley: Univ. of California Pr., 1946), p.43.

22. S.P.G. Record Books, 4:188, S.P.G. Archives mss., London (Francis Lister Hawkes transcriptions).

23. *South Carolina Gazette,* April 15, 1732.

24. Trott, *Laws,* p.90–94 (*See* Chapter 5, note 18).

25. North Carolina, *Colonial Records,* 1:860.

26. *Ibid.,* 2:128, 130, 144.

27. Sion College mss., p.285–92.

28. Francis Greenwood, *A History of King's Chapel* (Boston: Carter, 1833), p.55.

29. "Remarks by the Rev. J. W. Foote," *Massachusetts Historical Society Proceedings* (Boston: The Society, 1880–81), 18:424.

30. *Ibid.*, p.425.

31. U.S. Bureau of Education, *Public Libraries in the United States of America: Their History, Condition and Management*. Special Report, pt. 1 (Washington, D.C.: Government Printing Office, 1876), p.34.

32. Josiah Quincey, *History of the Athenaeum* (Cambridge, Mass.: Metcalf, 1851), p.88.

33. *Ibid.*, p.58.

34. Foote, "Remarks," p.426.

35. Bray, Bibliotheca Provincialis Americanae, p.52, S.P.G. Archives mss. (UCLA photocopy).

36. *Ibid.*, p.55.

37. *Ibid.*, p.164.

38. *Ibid.*, p.4.

39. Trinity Parish, Vestry Minutes, 1:200. Ms. in Trinity Church Vestry, New York.

40. S.P.G. Letter Book, no. 112 (1702–99), S.P.G. Archives mss., London. Copies of these Letter Books, made by Francis Lister Hawkes, are now in the New-York Historical Society Library.

41. Trinity Parish, Vestry Minutes, 1:38.

42. *Ibid.*, p.58.

43. New York (State), *Colonial Documents* (Albany: J. Munsell, 1866–72), 4:1182.

44. Trinity Parish, Vestry Minutes, 1:210–12, 218–20. Elliston's donations would have brought the collection up to a total of at least 382 volumes.

45. *Ibid.*, p.398.

46. The letter is quoted in full in Perry, *History of the American Episcopal Church*, 1:464.

47. Perry, *Historical Collections*, 2:11.

48. *Correspondence Between William Penn and James Logan, Secretary of the Province of Pennsylvania, and Others, 1700–1750* (Philadelphia: Historical Society, 1870–72), 1:124–25.

49. Perry, *History of the American Episcopal Church*, 1:230.

50. *Pennsylvania Magazine of History and Biography* (Philadelphia: Historical Society, 1880), 45:296.

51. *Ibid.*, p.297.

52. *Ibid.*, p.298.

53. *Ibid.*, p.299.

Chapter 7

1. Bibliotheca Provincialis Americanae, p.9, Ms. in S.P.G. Archives, London.

2. *Ibid.*, p.3.

3. Archives of Maryland, *Proceedings of the Council of Maryland, 1696–1698* (Baltimore: Historical Society, 1903), 23:177.

4. Probably the best single article on the Maryland libraries is that by Bernard C. Steiner in the *American Historical Review* (1896–97), 2:59–75. Further material

is presented in his *The Reverend Thomas Bray and His Work Relating to Maryland* (Baltimore: Historical Society, 1901).

5. U.S. Office of Education, *Public Libraries*, p.3–4.

6. *Calendar of State Papers*, Col. Ser. *Am. & W.I.*, p.717–18 (May 15, 1696–Oct. 31, 1697).

7. Bray, Accounts, pt. 2, p.4.

8. *Ibid.*, pt. 1, p.11.

9. *Ibid.*, p.5.

10. *Ibid.*, p.7.

11. *Ibid.*, pt. 2, p.5.

12. *Ibid.*, p.6.

13. North Carolina, *Colonial Records*, 2:128.

14. *Ibid.*, p.130.

15. Bray, Accounts, pt. 2, p.3.

16. *Ibid.*, p.5.

17. *Ibid.*, p.4.

18. *Ibid.*, p.4. The men were Meurson, a schoolmaster, and Steward, a minister. They were later supported by the S.P.G.

19. Thomas Bray, *Several Circular Letters to the Clergy of Maryland*, p.13.

20. *Ibid.*, p.14.

21. *Ibid.*, p.20.

22. Gambrall, *Church Life in Colonial Maryland*, p.104–11.

23. Bray, Accounts, *passim*.

24. North Carolina, *Colonial Records*, 2:123, 153.

Chapter 8

1. "Charter of the S.P.G., Section I," S.P.G. *A Collection of Papers, Printed by Order of the Society for the Propagation of the Gospel in Foreign Parts* (London: E. Owen, 1741), p.1–3.

2. Peter Force, *Tracts and Other Papers. . .* (New York: Peter Smith, 1947), 1:1.

3. *Colonial Society of Massachusetts Publications*, 28:107–75 (1935).

4. "Charter of the S.P.G.," p.3. The best modern account is William Kellaway, *The New England Company* (London: Longmans, 1961).

5. William Allen and Edmund McClure, *Two Hundred Years: The History of the S.P.C.K.* (London: S.P.C.K., 1898), p.8.

6. *Ibid.*, p.9.

7. *Ibid.*, p.11.

8. Sion College mss., p.242–43.

9. *Ibid.*, p.494.

10. Allen and McClure, *Two Hundred Years*, p.43.

11. *Ibid.*, p.226.

12. *Ibid.*, p.491.

13. *Ibid.*, p.122.

14. *Ibid.*, p.495. The S.P.G. took over the foreign work.

15. *Ibid.*, p.78.

16. William Lowther-Clarke, *History of the S.P.C.K.* (London: S.P.C.K., 1959), p.79, 81.

17. *Parochial Libraries of the Church of England*, p.48–50 (*See* Chapter 2, note 25).

18. *Dictionary of American Biography*, 8:463.

19. William Lowther-Clarke, *Eighteenth Century Piety* (London: S.P.C.K., 1944), p.40.

20. Henry Fuller, "The Philosophical Apparatus of Yale College," *Papers in Honor of Andrew Keogh* (New Haven: privately printed, 1938), p.163–80. Also, Anne Pratt, "Books Sent from England by Jeremiah Dummer to Yale College," *ibid.*, p.8–14.

21. *Yale University Library Gazette*, 8:5 (1946).

22. Thomas Clap, *The Annals, or History of Yale College* (New Haven, Conn.: Hotchkiss, Mecom, 1776), p.47.

23. Allen and McClure, *Two Hundred Years*, p.29.

Chapter 9

1. *History of the Convocation of the Prelates and Clergy of the Province of Canterbury, 1700* (London: n.p., 1702), p.243.

2. Lowther-Clarke, *History of the S.P.C.K.*, p.8.

3. S.P.C.K. Journal, Nov. 4 and 18, 1701, S.P.C.K. Archives mss., London.

4. S.P.G. Journal, 1:13.

5. James Anderson, *History of the Church of England in the Colonies and Foreign Dependencies* (London: Rivington, 1856), 2:409.

6. "Charter of the S.P.G.," p.837.

7. George Keith, *A Journal of Travels from New Hampshire to Curatuck, on Continent of North America* (London: William Downing, 1706).

8. "Charter of the S.P.G.," p.79–80.

9. Allen and McClure, *Two Hundred Years*, p.41.

10. *Ibid.*, p.42.

11. Perry, *History of the American Episcopal Church*, 1:596.

12. *Ibid.*, p.598.

13. S.P.G. Letter Book, no. 16, pp.126–27. Mossom's letter included a catalog of the library showing 37 volumes.

14. S.P.G. Letter Book, "Replies of the American Clergy," p.127.

15. S.P.G. Proceedings, 14:221, S.P.G. Archives mss., London.

16. *Ibid.*, 12:469.

17. *Ibid.*, p.573.

18. *Ibid.*, 23:109–10.

19. *Life and Times of Edward Bass* (Boston: Houghton Mifflin, 1897), p.176.

20. Nicholas Hoppin, *Sermon on the Re-Opening of Christ Church, Cambridge* (Boston: Ide and Dutton, 1858), p.72.

21. *Library of Christ Church, Boston* (Boston: Merrymount Pr., 1917), p.25.

22. *Ibid.*, p.13–14.

23. *Ibid.*, p.21.

24. *Ibid.*, p.27.

25. *Historical Collections of South Carolina*, comp. by B. R. Carroll (New York: Harper, 1856), p.567.

26. North Carolina, *Colonial Records*, 1:712.

27. *Ibid.*, 2:55, 123, 128.

28. Perry, *Historical Collections*, vol. 3, *Pennsylvania*, p.133, 141, 296.

29. Perry, *Historical Collections*, vol. 4, *Maryland*, p.302.

30. North Carolina, *Colonial Records*, 4:13.

31. Although there were dozens of libraries established by the S.P.G. in the

colonies, most of them were quite similar in content. There were nineteen libraries in Connecticut, eight in New York, eight in Pennsylvania, two in Delaware, and one in Portsmouth, New Hampshire, at St. John's church.

32. George Hills, *History of the Church in Burlington, New Jersey* (Trenton: Sharp, 1876), p.83.

33. Piper was also a lay reader in the church.

34. Hills, *History of the Church in Burlington*, p.421. The list of effects of Dr. Wharton included "Books, $280."

Chapter 10

1. Associates of the Late Doctor Bray, *Minutes*, 3:6, S.P.G. Archives mss., London.

2. Letter from Coram to Benjamin Coleman, Apr. 30, 1734, *Massachusetts Historical Society Proceedings* (1923), 61:19. Coleman was pastor of the Brattle Church in Boston, and influential in securing the Hollis and Holden gifts for Harvard College. Verner W. Crane, in *The Southern Frontier* (Durham, N.C.: Duke Univ., 1929), chapter 13, believes that Bray had a great deal to do with the plans for founding the colony of Georgia.

3. John Lydekker, "Thomas Bray, Founder of Missionary Enterprise," *Historical Magazine of the Protestant Episcopal Church*, 12:32 (1943).

4. Bray Associates, *Minutes*, 3:6.

5. Historical Manuscripts Commission, *Manuscripts of the Earl of Egmont. Diary, 1730–33* (London: His Majesty's Stationery Office, 1920), 1:120–64, 209, 218.

6. *Ibid.*, p.382.

7. Letter from Thomas Coram to Benjamin Coleman, Apr. 30, 1734, *Massachusetts Historical Society Publications*, 61:21.

8. Egmont, *Diary*, 2:182. The library to the Palatine minister probably went to Germanna, the settlement on the Rappahannock founded by Governor Spotswood. The Palatine settlement, near what is now the city of Harrisonburg, was not founded until 1740, by settlers from Pennsylvania.

9. Perry, *History of the American Colonial Church*, 2:235.

10. Egmont, *Diary*, 2:268.

11. *Ibid.*, p.344.

12. Associates of the Late Doctor Bray, *An Account of Books Sent Abroad by the Associates of the Late Doctor Bray to Clergymen and Others in America to Encourage and Assist them in the Conversion of the Negroes to Christianity, 1753–1807*, p.6, S.P.G. Archives mss., London.

13. Parochial libraries were sent to Savannah, Georgia; Charleston, South Carolina; Orange and King George counties, Germanna, and Leeds, Virginia; Woodbridge, New Jersey; and Wilmington, North Carolina.

14. Bray Associates, Dr. Bray's Accounts (1699–1702), *passim*, S.P.G. Archives mss., London.

15. Bray Associates, Abstracts of Proceedings, p.7, S.P.G. Archives mss., London.

16. *Ibid.*, p.11.

17. *Pennsylvania Magazine of History and Biography* 73:301–45 (1949).

18. Albert Smyth, *The Works of Benjamin Franklin* (New York: Macmillan, 1905–7), 4:23.

19. Bray Associates, Abstracts, p.17.

20. Bray Associates, Accounts, p.26.
21. Bray Associates, Abstracts, p.24.
22. *Ibid.*, p.27. For the contents of the library, see appendix B.
23. *Ibid.*, p.31.
24. Bray Associates, Accounts, p.152.
25. *Notes and Queries* 152:381 (1927). There were 176 libraries in 1877.

Index

DATE DUE